TOXICITY AT THE WORKPLACE

HOW CAN YOU PROTECT YOURSELF FROM TOXIC COWORKERS, BOSSES, AND A WORKPLACE CULTURE THAT DRAINS YOUR TALENT?

DR. AMIT DAS

To

All my bosses and mentors who made a difference in my professional career.

"According to the Society for Human Resource Management, 58% of departing employees attribute the toxic workplace culture to their supervisors. A toxic workplace is frequently brought about by toxic managers. Workplace toxicity is at the centre of most company conversations due to large-scale layoffs, reorganisations, high turnover, poor leadership, workplace bullying, etc. If you're not satisfied at work, it may spill over into your personal life and impair your relationships with friends and family, as well as your physical and emotional health. Remember, a key element of a profitable business operation is establishing and maintaining a safe and productive work environment."

- Dr. Amit Das, Motivational Speaker, Leadership Coach , Counsellor, and Mentor.

Contents

Foreword

Dear Reader,

Thank you for taking the time to learn more about **"TOXICITY AT THE WORKPLACE"** and the rewarding outcome of increasing your personal productivity. This is a book with a stunning design that is packed with clear, actionable guidance on how to spot and address toxic people, habits, and work environments. Checklists, and examples from the real world are all included to help you learn what to look for and how to react.

You may handle stress in a hostile work environment and safeguard yourself from the detrimental effects of office politics by reading this book. It will assist you in controlling toxic employees, personalities, and habits. You'll discover how to succeed in workplace politics, prevent depression and burnout, and avoid both. A poisonous atmosphere may be changed into a high-minded society where contentment prevails over resentment, hope over despair, affirmation over judgement, and collaboration over anarchy. Whether you are a senior executive or a regular employee, work for a large corporation or own a small business, we all have something to learn. This book is for you if you're one of those dejected workers (at any level in the company) who feels that your workplace is robbing you of your life.

This book, **"TOXICITY AT THE WORKPLACE"** will walk you through the steps necessary to implement and maintain a good change in the workplace. With the help of this book, you'll discover how to foster a work climate that reflects your beliefs and keeps negativity from growing. Inside, you'll learn how to...

- Recognise the characteristics that make or break a team.
- Establish a secure atmosphere that promotes openness.
- Form transcendent team relationships quickly.

This book highlights indicators of a toxic workplace and provides advice for dealing with toxicities at work (e.g., toxic employees, toxic leaders, and a toxic culture). If you believe that your workplace is toxic, you must find long-term solutions to make it a healthier place to work before it obliterates you. Use the advice in this book to change a toxic work environment so that it benefits both you and your workplace. You will be able to identify and address your own problematic workplace behaviours with the support of your own toxic work behaviors. This small yellow book, which is a part of a larger series that examines how to achieve success in a healthy way, will help you let go of negative behaviours and poisonous inclinations and replace them with good ones that can advance your career and the lives of others around you.

This book intends to further the conversation on the significance of an employee's mental health, which is frequently disregarded these days. It highlights the telltale indicators of a toxic workplace, allowing an employee to decide between fighting the system by becoming well-versed in it or leaving or quitting the company to pursue mental tranquility. This book concludes with some advice for workers on how to safeguard their crucial sense of tranquility. Additionally, it's a crucial chance for organisations to acknowledge how internal politics are harming their reputation. The author also pledges to continue discussing it until the problem is properly identified and amicably resolved.

This book offers practical advice on how to stay alive in a hostile work environment. You could even relate to some of the humorous examples. If you decide to leave your toxic employment, this book also offers practical advice you may use to make the transition successfully. This book looks at the crucial role that HR professionals play in their companies as "toxin handlers" and the risks they run while handling toxic workplace feelings brought on by challenging organisational decisions like mergers and acquisitions, layoffs, and restructuring. It explores what they do, why they do it, and the benefits the job brings to their personal and professional lives. It also looks at the hazards to their personal safety that they face.

This book emphasises the delicate balancing act that HR must perform in order to care for employees and support their causes while also advancing the business goals established by senior management. The author explores the costs to toxin handlers' individual well-being while illustrating how they lessen organisational suffering at difficult times. Readers will discover how to lessen the harmful effects of toxic emotions on both an organisational and personal level.

This book outlines the typical difficulties of a toxic workplace and provides a road map for converting toxic workplaces into winning workplaces that bring out the best in both people and companies! Change your concentration to alter your ideas, which will alter your feelings, which will alter how you communicate with the outside world, and your decision to alter will alter what you draw to you. Use the advice in this book to change a toxic work environment so that it benefits both you and your workplace. If you believe that your workplace is toxic, you must find long-term solutions to make it a healthier place to work before it obliterates you.

This book gives you easy-to-implement strategies you can take to improve your working environment right away. What should you do if your employer is tough or toxic? Learn to work with your manager to support your preferred working methods. This book is for those who don't require expert assistance and can manage and get rid of their job anxiety on their own. This book teaches you how to set up appropriate boundaries that will keep you happy and productive and offers great tactics for dealing with coworkers who like to start workplace drama. With the help of this book you'll discover practical, step-by-step methods for handling obnoxious coworkers, and you could even see where and how you've made mistakes in the past.

Here, in this book the author, Dr. Amit Das outlines multuple ways in this extremely comprehensive, no-fluff book how toxic emotions may infiltrate the workplace, sometimes sneaking up on you before rearing their ugly heads and wrecking havoc on the whole workforce.

This book provides parents with an approachable way to support their childrens in thriving despite the negative forces of contemporary culture, despite the fact that the trip through modern parenthood may be hard and even perilous.

This book is jam-packed with advice, insider knowledge, and methods to help you deal with the difficulties of working in a toxic environment. It contains a list of indicators that you may use to convince your manager that the environment at work is poisonous. Examples of unethical behaviour in the workplace are also provided, along with suggestions for how to handle it. This book is for you if you're struggling in a toxic job and are ready to take charge of your career and your life. Leaders who are inclusive may prevent toxic workplaces.

You'll learn to recognise toxic personalities and to identify the behaviours and strategies of leaders who frequently fail. At the individual, team, and organisational levels, this book offers practical methods that integrate with research-based tactics. New perspectives on how leaders lead, corporate cultures thrive, and teams manage toxic personalities will be offered by "**TOXICITY AT THE WORKPLACE.**"

The insights in this book will help you get through everything, so you can succeed at work no matter how challenging the environment may be. This includes dealing with negativity and criticism from coworkers, finding ways to stay motivated, and overcoming unforeseen circumstances like losing your job. Read this book to get the freedom to live your own life and make your own decisions if you're surrounded by the world's takers. The exercises and insights in this book will help you get through everything, so you can succeed at work no matter how challenging the environment may be. Finally, you will discover his tried-and-true structure for creating a high-performing team that lasts in the book that follow not just for revenue and output but ultimately to save everyone on the team's life.

All those points have been captured in this part of the book to show what his mentors and well-wishers feel about this book and have shared their thoughts to make it an effective piece of advice for your success.

Thank you for taking the time to read this book. This practical book offers advice for workers trying to stay productive and focused when dealing with problematic coworkers in challenging situations, as well as for company leaders and HR experts looking to maintain a calm workplace. Additionally, the author provides examples of toxic cultures and suggestions for changing them, while also highlighting the tremendous successes that may be attained when people can work together productively.

Carpe diem.

Dr. Amit Das

Leadership Coach , Counsellor, and Mentor.

Preface

"When a workplace becomes toxic, its poison spreads beyond its walls and into the lives of its workers and their families."

According to the Society for Human Resource Management, 58% of departing employees attribute the toxic workplace culture to their supervisors. But hold out for now! Your resource for survival is this book. It's not just you. An unhealthy work environment may be very taxing and discouraging.

- **Do you find it difficult to function in a hazardous workplace?**
- **Do you feel like you are at war with angry, deceptive, and harmful coworkers, supervisors, or employees all the time?**

If so, continue reading.
In the office, it may sometimes seem as though you are always treading on thin ice. Do the workplace politics and bad vibes make you dread going to work? This book, which adopts a comprehensive approach, provides a concise description of how toxic cultures emerge and demonstrates how they may be fixed with actionable tips for organisations. I will provide solutions for needed change that can be implemented and is based on research in organisational and individual psychology.

Although it would be lovely to live in a perfect world, business cannot be conducted there. As a result, many people despise their jobs and are tired of working in a toxic environment. Most people accept that they can't improve their situation and choose to work within the unsatisfactory company culture. People don't act like programmable things and aren't robots. Executives and management frequently overlook that. But for every firm to reach its full potential, people are essential.

Many entrepreneurs who are growing their businesses are concerned that they could lose skilled workers or possibly be sued for discrimination, but they aren't yet ready to establish a complete human resources department. Leaders who are inclusive may prevent toxic workplaces. One of the last things you want to hear when you own a fantastic business that is improving the world is that a worker is experiencing harassment or discrimination. However, data show that harassment and discrimination are fairly common, and even well-known companies are not immune. There is a way to create a workplace that is more effective and healthy. This book will walk you through the steps necessary to implement and maintain a good change in the workplace.

Your organisation's common set of values, attitudes, and beliefs make up your corporate culture. It affects the kinds of applicants you recruit for available positions and is reflected in how you treat your clients and staff. Increased employee engagement, lower turnover, and higher productivity are all benefits of a good corporate culture. Create the necessary component for powerful groups. Steer clear of errors that undermine the team-first approach.

You're attempting to get through a challenging workday. It seems like you could be working in a harmful setting. Are you aware that being negative at work may seriously harm your health and personal life? Even though you may have heard a lot about toxic workplaces, have you ever considered the possibility that you may be contributing to the issue? Every employee in a company, including you, has poor habits, vices, and undesirable behaviours that affect the culture of the whole workplace.

Workplace toxicity is at the centre of most company conversations due to large-scale layoffs, reorganisations, high turnover, poor leadership, workplace bullying, etc. If you're not satisfied at work, it may spill over into your personal life and impair your relationships with friends and family, as well as your physical and emotional health. While most people would like to believe that they conduct themselves in a positive manner most of the time, especially at work, everyone has the capacity to slide into negative behaviours that can negatively affect their coworkers, their morale, and the organisation they work for. The many good and bad work behaviours people engage in, as well as the reasons behind them, are examined in this book.

A toxic work environment marked by bullying, harassment, victimisation, false accusations made by line managers against a group of employees they believed were critical to the status quo, and a sickening subculture of cover-ups by the HR department, which handled court cases and complaints. You might have experienced employees who recounted their investigations into systemic bullying and harassment that is ignored out of fear of the consequences, and staff no longer adheres to the policies and procedures created with the help of those who are supposed to protect a team of employees.

On a daily basis, many workers deal with the realities of abusive managers, toxic coworkers, and soul-crushing cultures. This book on toxic workplace presents real accounts from current employees who discuss how they survive, adapt, or leave. They talk openly about their experiences, regrets, and strategies for building resilience. Conflict, anxiety, and fury are abundant in toxic groups. People respond physiologically to their surroundings as though they are in a fight-or-flight scenario. The whistleblower policy is ineffective as well; it is characterised by corruption and cover-ups, and for many social persons who have experienced bullying, stopping and reporting to top management is the best course of action. The goal of this book is to encourage victims of bullying to speak up and protect others from experiencing the same cruelty at their workplace.

A toxic workplace is frequently brought about by toxic managers and leaders. Workplace toxicity is on the rise, and more individuals are speaking out about it. Toxic workplaces are frequently characterised by unrest, rivalry, low morale, constant pressure, negativity, turnover, harassment, and even bullying. The toxic boss is intended to help you keep your sanity and sense of self amidst workplace toxicity. But until circumstances change or until you decide to go on, you may discover methods to manage it.

If workplace cultural issues feel like a test you didn't realise you signed up for, The inclusive leader's to create a healthy workplace culture is a cheat sheet for passing it and fostering cultural health in your organisation.

Would you like to work for a company with a better corporate culture?

In the modern workplace, events like layoffs, harassment, discrimination, personality problems, or an abusive boss are just a few examples of the many things that may cause employees to feel significant emotional distress, including emotions of rage, tension, disappointment, and even terror. Although these kinds of occurrences are regrettably foreseeable and, in some ways, unavoidable, how firms address them—or don't—can cause major issues for employees. HR frequently has the duty to assist distressed workers in lessening their emotional suffering so that they can focus again and return to work as soon as possible, leading to favourable organisational outcomes. The tactics taught in this book will help HR professionals prepare for and deal with the organisational toxicity brought on by some of the unavoidable and challenging people-related circumstances they are going to encounter.

This book will help you identify common types of difficult coworkers and offer advice on how to deal with each of them productively. These coworkers include the insecure boss, the know-it-all peer, the biassed coworker, and others. No matter who you're in conflict with, I will impart concepts that will enable you to change the situation. It's challenging to take the high road, but I will provide you with a critical viewpoint on the importance of professional relationships as well as the understanding, support, and skills you need to succeed—on your terms. This book is a vital resource for navigating your most challenging professional relationships—and developing interpersonal resilience in the process. It is packed with relatable, occasionally embarrassing examples, the most recent behavioural science research, and helpful advice you can put to immediate use.

Everyone deserves respect and the right to be themselves, thus this shouldn't be the case. No matter what their origin or colour, every employee deserves respect.

Because of the complexity of the job and the fierce rivalry to excel, expectations from our coworkers and the immediate supervisor can leave unsightly scars on our attempts to advance. Sadly, workplace bullying sometimes seems subtle, but it somehow manifests itself within us, creating adversaries at work. At work, you have a right to be free from harassment of any type, including bullying and belittling. This book in your hands has provided helpful advice on how to handle conflicts at work effectively while avoiding or at least minimising adversaries. Additionally, you'll learn how to approach difficulties with the proper mindset. Personal work, experiences, and other real-life occurrences that altered my view on work, people, and society are included on its pages.

People are aware that toxic workplace situations are bad for business, but they are unaware of the extent of the harm being done and how to repair it. Everything will go wrong if you concentrate on believing that it will. Therefore, if you can shift your emphasis to the idea that you have complete control over your actions, you can choose to trust yourself and support yourself in making decisions about your thoughts and feelings. This will give you the confidence you need to make decisions about your job.

You're attempting to get through a challenging workday. It seems like you could be working in a harmful setting. Are you aware that being negative at work may seriously harm your health and personal life? If you believe that your workplace is toxic, you must find long-term solutions to make it a healthier place to work before it obliterates you. Use the advice in this book to change a toxic work environment so that it benefits both you and your workplace.

I hope that this book will serve not only as a present but also as a starting point for those difficult conversations that are inevitable in any workplace. The work's funny tone makes it feasible to approach problems that can be difficult to tackle head-on. Between being committed to your profession and being a workaholic, there are fine lines. Of course, there are times when working longer hours is necessary to complete a major assignment. But eventually, you'll start to feel like you're drowning. This book offers a fresh perspective that lowers workplace stress.

This book will teach you: Who to trust at work? How to dispel cognitive fallacies that cause stress, worry, and longer hours? Why you are more likely to develop depression if you are unfamiliar with the culture of your company? This book also teaches you time management skills and how to break bad behaviours that result in an overworked lifestyle.

You may safeguard yourself from politics and scheming with the aid of the guide. To increase your enjoyment and effectiveness, start right away with a little action.

At work, you may develop your strength, productivity, and sense of fulfillment. This book explains it to you. This book's description of workplace anxiety can help you pinpoint the areas of your job where you're experiencing difficulties. What about rivalry and conflict among coworkers? While keeping your job, there are a few simple strategies to strengthen your connections with your coworkers, reduce stress, and increase productivity at work. In this book the topic covered on anxiety caused by the worry of losing your work. By empowering yourself and demonstrating the value you provide, you may put yourself in a position to either save your current position or find a new one swiftly.

Dysfunction workplace is like an obtrusive ambiance. It influences you gently and is constantly present. Even if it's not negatively affecting your mood to the point where you're considering leaving yet, it's crucial to take control of the issue before it spirals out of control. It goes without saying that cocky jerks at work are poisonous and discouraging. I will describe in this book how to protect oneself from bullies that denigrate, criticise, and drain the vitality of others. You know who they are—the ones that cast disparaging glances during conferences or incite disputes via email without cause. You can avoid becoming depressed by the office drama even if you have no influence over it. This book provides a simple, effective method for dealing with difficult people, ranging from persistent whiners to laziness.

From the #MeToo movement, it's evident that abusive employers and deeply ingrained discriminatory practises are more common than ever in the workplace. The office has become a hotspot of social poison. Such behaviour is not only morally repugnant and harmful to its victims, but it also lowers productivity, increases staff turnover, and frequently tarnishes an organisation's overall brand. Use the strategies that have been shown to transform employees' negative emotions into positive ones in order to convince your bosses and coworkers to join you on the high morale, high productivity train once and for all. Don't allow a bully to steal your joy from life.

Emotionally toxic environments are common, pervasive, affect a huge number of people, and harm both organisations and individuals. If you've ever worked in a setting where a bully intimidates you and brings a host of poisonous feelings to the office, you know how quickly a positive attitude can be destroyed and any productivity for the day killed.

Confusion, disorientation, physical health issues, and sadness ensue. You, your workplace, family, and friends are all impacted by this. Now is the time to figure out what to do. This book, which is based on cutting-edge research, provides parents with the techniques they need to provide their daughters with the life skills they need to fend off harmful cultural influences. This book distils the issues and root causes of toxic environments before attacking the problem head-on, drawing on his decades of experience in HR and mediation.

One of the last things you want to hear when you own a fantastic business that is improving the world is that a worker is experiencing harassment or discrimination. However, data show that harassment and discrimination are fairly common, and even well-known companies are not immune. Many entrepreneurs who are growing their businesses are concerned that they could lose skilled workers or possibly be sued for discrimination, but they aren't yet ready to establish a complete human resources department.

- **How to ensure that you quickly determine whether a significant issue is there while avoiding wasting all of your time listening to complaints?**
- **Why investigations alone are insufficient to address workplace complaints?**
- **How to deal with employee problems well (without losing good employees)?**

- **Why it's important for every employee to learn how to comprehend and deal with power dynamics in the workplace?**

This book is a revolutionary investigation into how the best organisations function that will alter the way we think and cooperate. It combines cutting-edge science, on-the-ground knowledge, and useful suggestions for action. If workplace cultural issues feel like a test you didn't realise you signed up for, this book is a cheat sheet for passing it and fostering cultural health in your organisation.

It offers helpful advice for handling difficult circumstances at work. Additionally, it provides a thorough explanation of several toxic personalities that might aid you in averting future problems. This book includes a clear presentation, helpful advice, and an in-depth explanation. This book is a fun and interesting read, whether you're interested in learning more about people's personalities or have a problem with toxic coworkers.

Leaders who are inclusive may prevent toxic workplaces.

One of the last things you want to hear when you own a fantastic business that is improving the world is that a worker is experiencing harassment or discrimination. However, data show that harassment and discrimination are fairly common, and even well-known companies are not immune. The book offers readers helpful advice on how to handle issues at work and foster an inclusive environment. Effective management, corporate governance, and professional development are all benefited by transformational leadership. The book offers detailed guidance on how to avoid drama-producing situations as well as useful information on:

- Becoming an organisation that values and practises freedom, fearlessness, and fairness.
- Anticipating drama-producing situations and using emotional intelligence to speak more clearly and persuasively about delicate, contentious issues in the workplace.

The days of a single genius working alone in a corner to think up the next great novel idea are long gone. Today, collaboration is prioritised. Getting along with coworkers and friends outside of the office offers several benefits, including greater idea generation, increased employee happiness, and a positive influence on an individual's capacity for innovation without strain as well as that of the group or organisation. It discusses how to choose relationships that are healthy, how to create clear boundaries, and how to see warning signs that should make us steer clear of a certain person. Whether you are dealing with a sociopathic coworker, a bullying employer, or a narcissistic partner, there is useful information that may help you not only protect but also improve your mental health. You will understand the characteristics of a poisonous workplace and how to survive there if necessary. Read this book to get the freedom to live your own life and make your own decisions if you're surrounded by the world's takers. This includes dealing with negativity and criticism from coworkers, finding ways to stay motivated, and overcoming unforeseen circumstances like losing your job.

Relations at work may be challenging. Our creativity and productivity suffer, we become less able to reason rationally and make wise judgements, and we get disengaged when dealing with challenging individuals. We might stress ourselves to sleep, stop working, or act in ways we later regret, like rolling our eyes in a meeting, yelling at coworkers, or being silent when we should have spoken up. We grin and bear things much too frequently, acting as though we had no other option. Or give up because one-size-fits-all fixes haven't succeeded. You can only put up with so much careless, unreasonable, or spiteful conduct, though; you also have to think about your job and mental health.

I speak on subjects including establishing boundaries, getting help, fostering resilience, and learning how to speak up for oneself and others at work. The book's ultimate purpose is to provide readers with the tools they need to take charge of their own health and discover methods to flourish in spite of the difficulties they encounter in their toxic environments.

"Always keep in mind that a supportive workplace is the ideal setting for original thought and idea development. Low staff engagement, hindered innovation, and excessive employee turnover are all caused by toxic bosses." - Dr. Amit Das

Acknowledgements

At the outset, I will thank my family for supporting me throughout the journey of writing my book and encouraging me to live my dreams; my son has always been instrumental in giving his inspiration to complete the writing of this book. Despite the fact that I am listed as the author of this book, **"TOXICITY AT THE WORKPLACE"** *would not have been published if I had depended entirely on my own talents. Creating this book required more than anything—it took a family of dedicated and caring people who were always prepared to lend a hand.*

Writing a book while working full-time is no simple task, so I'd want to express my gratitude to my amazing coworkers who act as cheerleaders in equal measure. Thank you, too, to my students and clients for your patience and unflinching support while I worked on this book!

Thank you to everyone who has listened to me argue for doing everything you can to make your life, including your work life, more progressive. I appreciate everyone's assistance throughout the process. This book would not have been possible without each of you having had an impact on my life in some manner.

Lastly, I would like to thank all the people with whom I have been associated. You gave me power. I would like to thank Notion Press for publishing my book. Finally, thank you all for gifting your time to read this book.

I'd want to convey my heartfelt appreciation to the almighty God for bestowing his blessings and being so gracious.

CHAPTER ONE

Rebuilding Respect and Tolerance in a Toxic Workplace

"All of us are surrounded by toxic individuals that make our lives miserable. If a person discovers negative individuals in his life, he should work on improving his own nature rather than that of others, since his own fundamental foundation determines how poisonous or acidic the environment around him is."

Are you afraid to go to work?

Dealing with obnoxious coworkers, difficult supervisors, and irate clients can have an impact on how well you perform at work. No one can afford to lose their employment now, given the tough economic conditions. We work for half of our waking hours, yet we almost never pause to think about the psychological or emotional toll it takes on us. For many people, the workplace is like a second home. Your team is likely the group you spend more time with than your family or friends.

The workplace of the twenty-first century is an example of several people working together for a shared commercial objective. Employers must reconstitute their teams in the end of the year 2023 so that they can "strike the ground running" after the economy has recovered. Believing that the staff members are prepared to collaborate with one another in a moral and courteous way and that their shared goal will be productivity rather than conflict.

"Toxic people will pollute everything around them. Don't hesitate. Fumigate."

According to the Greek mythology and the term "toxikon," which means poison or arrow venom, are the origins of the word "toxic." Toxic can imply "poisonous" or "producing unpleasant sensations; damaging or malevolent," according to one definition. Toxicology in the workplace can take many different forms. It can range from harassment or bullying to a business that participates in unethical behaviour and is dishonest with its staff. Of course, poison is not just present in the physical workplace. It can also be the harassment against remote employees occurs via email, video calls, phone conversations, and chat applications.

Another sign of a toxic workplace is low compensation, a lack of recognition or reward for great performance, a focus on customers over people, a lack of internal mobility, a lack of employee voice, a breach of trust, or a culture that continuously blurs the lines between work and personal life. And far too frequently, these issues begin at the top.

If you're not satisfied with your workplace, it may affect other areas of your life as well, harming your long-term success, self-confidence, and self-esteem. The increased stress of working in a dysfunctional office can cause job burnout, weariness, listlessness, and depression. Toxic workplaces can also have an effect on your health. There are different levels of dysfunction in every company. For instance, you can enjoy your work a lot yet be in charge of a very chaotic team. That may also be the case if there is persistent disagreement in your workplace that is out of your control.

A toxic work environment is one where management methods, procedures, and rules are prevalent and encourage unproductive behaviours and disagreements among team members. Employees may suffer as a result, since it may hinder their ability to be productive and advance their careers. Ineffective corporate cultures may also result in employee discontent and dissatisfaction, which motivates them to search for other employment.

"Pay no attention to toxic words. What people say is often a reflection of themselves, not you."

On one level, a toxic work environment is institutional-centric, meaning that the organisation's policies and procedures were created with the firm in mind rather than the employees. Ineffective work practises, such as the demand that workers work from the office, are another sign of a toxic workplace culture. Similarly, it is common to see employees offered incentives and perks that are simple financially for the company but difficult for them personally. Workplace "illnesses," including poor team cohesiveness, increased absenteeism and tardiness, poorer productivity, and high turnover, are frequently brought on by toxic work cultures.

What does a toxic workplace entail?

It is possible for toxic supervisors to create an uncomfortable environment at work. That manager is poison if they consistently undermine your confidence, self-worth, and skills. Such supervisors completely misinterpret what leadership is, which creates a poisonous work atmosphere. What contributes to a poisonous workplace?

A common question is,

- **Who is responsible for workplace toxicity?**
- **Who needs to be held responsible?**
- **Do we blame high turnover rates for interfering with teamwork?**

A workplace is considered toxic when the tasks, people, and surroundings interfere with your life. Your physical health may be negatively impacted by these disturbances, which may cause restless nights, a feeling of perpetual alertness, sweaty palms, and a racing heart. Significant drama and internal conflict are signs of workplace toxicity when personal conflicts interfere with productivity.

"Surround yourself with positive individuals that support your goals, believe in your objectives, and inspire the best in you."

Any level of employee at your place of business has the potential to poison the workplace. Whether they are supervisors, friends, or low-level workers, Rapidly spreading office gossip and constant peer pressure may cause your employees to feel inadequate about their work. You're probably working in a toxic environment if your organisation hasn't done a good job of communicating its ideals. A sensation of widespread animosity is produced by bad policies or a code of behaviour that isn't followed. Mistrust is generated by managers' weak leadership and lack of communication. I consider poor leadership to be the root cause of a poisonous workplace culture. Additionally, one may check out Glassdoor reviews; if there are any unfavourable remarks, it is a sign of toxicity.

You may safeguard yourself from politics and scheming with the aid of the guide. To increase your enjoyment and effectiveness, start right away with a little action.

An eight-person team that handled employee benefits had been working together for a very long time at a company with 5,000 employees. When their manager retired, a new one was appointed, which completely upended the group. The group perceived this boss as picking one person and intimidating him or her until he or she resigned. He would then pick a new victim and harass her until she gave up. The former team had been dismantled, and this manager soon had eight new workers.

Can you connect the same situation with yours?

Why does bullying occur?

Why do things like bullying occur?

Let's first look at the bully. Although it may appear that bullying is done on purpose, that is simply untrue. Bullies act this way because they are extremely insecure. They live in terror of their mask of uber-competence being blown, which they desperately want to maintain. Bullies also lack social and emotional intelligence, which is the capacity to control one's own emotions as well as those of others. They also have poor communication abilities. They might be lacking in leadership abilities. They will engage in physical violence against others if they learn such tactics from past management. Additionally, they are unable to manage stress in a productive way.

Let's now examine the victims of bullying. To be clear, I am in no way pointing the finger at anyone or implying that they did something to warrant this conduct. However, bullying is a two-way interaction. Since it is a transaction, we must consider the function of the targets. First off, targets frequently do well. They put forth a lot of effort and find it incomprehensible why someone would treat them badly.

However, if a high performer has a manager who aspires to be thought of as supremely competent, that high performer poses a challenge to that management. The boss or management is concerned that this performer will overshadow them. The second is that the targeted don't defend themselves. If the target doesn't stand out for themselves during the initial bullying episode, when the bully is hostile, another act of hostility is certain to follow.

As time goes on, the target refuses to request an end to the conduct, and the bullying escalates in frequency and severity. The relationship eventually degenerates into one of imbalanced power. In reality, the victim of bullying has frequently explained it away by claiming that it is an expected aspect of working there.

Let's now examine the organisation. A lot of research has been done on the conditions that might make bullying more likely to occur, and some of these conditions include organisational change, competitive environments, bureaucracy, reward systems that are solely based on performance rather than behaviour, an unsatisfied workforce, and companies with a lot of intelligent or long-term employees. In my consulting work, I've also seen that firms that are not focused on their fundamental principles and culture appear to allow bullying to flourish.

Bullying also appears to occur in firms with compliance-focused HR and organisations where managers aren't trained to step in and set standards for behaviour. Bullying will also flourish in workplaces where onlookers stay silent. Why would they, too? Of course, they are afraid that if they do anything to enrage the bully, they may end up on his hit list. As the saying goes, "don't poke the bear."

However, that brings us to the final component of the puzzle. Bullying will flourish if individuals aren't taught and encouraged to report it. And who is in charge of educating and motivating them? Leaders. The workforce must be made aware that bullying and other bad actions will not be accepted, and leaders must take a strong stand in favour of creating a pleasant work environment. Actions are the only way to convey this message. Bullies who are great performers must nevertheless be censured, given coaching, or asked to leave, even if they are bullies. Leaders and managers ultimately need to promote respect so that individuals feel free to voice their opinions. And that is how bullying may be stopped.

Do you bully others?

All this discussion of bullying at work serves as a reminder to me that we must also be conscious of our own actions. It's simple to blame others and think that they are the only issue. Here are some of the behaviours I hear about—behaviors that any one of us may engage in—from the employees I've spoken with who work for bullying executives. If you lose your temper quickly at work, your coworkers may view you as a bully.

- **Do you notice that you become irritable with those who pester you with inquiries?**
- **Do you find it annoying to have to explain something again?**

Take a step back and make sure your voice is polite and businesslike. Do you ever wonder how the other person felt following a conversation? Do you ever feel like I should apologise because that could have been impolite? If you don't, your social and emotional intelligence may require some improvement. Bullies could also be thought of as those who holler. No matter how furious you are, yelling is never appropriate in a professional setting.

- **How do you resolve conflicts?**
- **Are they about coming to an agreement or about winning?**

It's necessary to take a step back and consider more efficient approaches to handling problems if you're focused on being correct and making sure you're heard. Maintaining an even tone, paraphrasing, and asking several questions are all crucial components of constructive conflict, as is making sure the other party feels heard. Alright, one more thing.

- **How do you react when someone makes a mistake or doesn't meet your standards?**
- **Do you micromanage others?**

Bullies sometimes assume that others are inept and point out mistakes or poor performance insensitively or harshly.

It may be important to establish and uphold personal boundaries if you frequently feel uncomfortable with how people treat you. Having clear boundaries can help ensure that your relationships are courteous, encouraging, and caring. Because you deserve to be treated well. They will inspire you to set boundaries for what is appropriate behaviour from those around you and will help you keep a safe distance from those who do not have your best interests at heart. If you allow them to, toxic individuals may make you feel uncomfortable. Recognise their conduct and keep your distance from them. And while communicating with them, emphasise the good. So, my questions to you are as follows:

- **How to comprehend your personality type and the personalities of the other team members?**
- **How to use humour to get through challenging conditions at work?**

- **How to recognise and deal with becoming entangled in a negative web?**
- **How to start releasing yourself from bad routines, perspectives, and dispositions that have fueled a poisonous workplace?**
- **Do you drag yourself out of bed in the morning to get to work?**

According to a report by Monster, 42% of Americans have quit their jobs as a result of an unduly stressful workplace. A job that makes your employees stressed out and frequently interferes with their time with friends and family is an indication of chronic stress. According to a poll conducted by the Families and Work Institute, 43% of workers who report feeling overworked severely or frequently express anger towards their bosses. Employees are frequently overburdened with duties when they operate in a hostile environment. Overworking oneself can result in serious burnout and resentment. A bad comapny culture shows red flags when:

- You don't have a set of guiding principles.
- There is a lot of workplace gossip.
- Employees are frequently missing or tardy.
- Employees frequently put in extra hours or skip lunch.
- Employers continue to prioritise culture fit.
- Lack of a DEI policy.
- No workplace giving programmes, little to no hiring from within, and employee public criticism.

Yes, bullying at work is a serious problem that many people deal with, but it is dealt with less frequently. Bullies are often bosses 61% of the time and peers 33% of the time.

Your organisation probably has a poisonous culture if going to work makes your workers feel burdened, terrified, and threatened.

Why do bullies bully?

Your response may be a resounding yes if you have experienced bullying. However, I have to admit that after working to stop bullying for ten years, the most of the time, it isn't. Therefore, give me a chance. There are two causes of bullying or abrasive behaviour. First, those who bully others have low levels of social and emotional intelligence. They are unaware of the negative consequences of their actions. They just don't get why they need to change, despite repeated warnings to this effect. As an illustration, I asked Rohit, one of my coaching clients, if he was prepared to participate in coaching when we first met. I think so, he said. I can't believe no one has informed me in three years while I've been walking around like this. I wish they hadn't held off telling me until I was ready to lose my job. But Rohit had heard this a lot. People had left or been moved directly in front of him, and HR and his boss had been attempting to replace him for a while. He simply didn't grasp it.

Second, the desire to be perceived as supremely capable drives those who bully others. They've somehow developed the belief that doing this will help them in their effort. Additionally, it unnerves them when they think others are incapable. If they perceive ineptitude around them, they get nervous about their own capacity to appear competent and lash out. In actuality, the majority of the clients I work with share a trait. They can comprehend information considerably more rapidly than the majority of people, thus it irritates them when others can't. They see this as ineptitude and think it causes them to move more slowly.

In addition to those two primary causes, people also bully because they picked it up from someone, whether they learnt it as a youngster or from a prior boss. Additionally, the group supports bullying. Every single individual I've worked with has encountered obstacles that have influenced their behaviour, such as an unorganised structure or unclear goals, intense competition, combative bosses, or a lack of HR assistance in dealing with employee performance. By rewarding high performers, who bullies typically are, or by having a leader who just tolerates the conduct, the company can also encourage bullying.

Bullying occurs everywhere, including in offices, schools, and political settings. Bullying at work refers to persistent victimisation that tilts the psychological balance of power in favour of the bullies. Targets find it difficult, if not impossible, to defend themselves because of the power disparity. Targets and witnesses alike have psychological issues as a result, such as tension, worry, and sadness. And as a result, bodily issues including headaches, heart issues, insomnia, and other issues arise. Naturally, those who are terrified of their employer or a coworker don't perform at their best, which affects both the productivity and calibre of their job.

Additionally affected are internal relationships, employee happiness, corporate loyalty, and customer service. Bullying may be fairly subtle, and it frequently starts with a minor slight or impolite email. There is a first instance of rudeness, but nobody complains. The lack of response implies that this behaviour is acceptable. With time, the actions multiply and escalate in frequency and aggression. If a strong, supportive culture isn't in place, targets and witnesses eventually learn that the bully has psychological power and feel powerless to stop the conduct. People are then more inclined to speak up. You might now be asking what distinguishes harassment from bullying. There is no response.

Look at the definition of harassment on the website of the Equal Employment Opportunity Commission. When engaging in the offensive behaviour becomes a requirement for keeping a job, or when it is severe or pervasive enough to produce a work atmosphere that a reasonable person would consider intimidating, hostile, or abusive, that behaviour is unacceptable. That is how bullying at work is described.

However, whether you include the section regarding race, colour, religion, sex, national origin, age, handicap, or genetic information, the law makes a distinction between the two. If you bully someone due to one or more of these protected qualities, you are breaking the law. That kind of bullying is considered harassment under the law. Conflict arises when two individuals disagree yet both believe they have a voice. However, when one person's behaviour gets so forceful that the other person hears them, the conflict might turn into bullying.

Now I have to ponder: Are you taking this course in order to find out if bullying occurs in your workplace? If it does, you may have some employees that feel severely hurt or even mistreated at work, and it's time to stop.

So, is bullying on purpose?

No. These folks don't get out of bed eager to make people weep. They set out in the morning with the intention of finishing the task, and they will do whatever it takes to make sure it is. But this is the reason the organisation must intervene. They will alter their behaviour if you can show them how their actions genuinely make them appear extremely inept. The longevity and commercial success of your firm depend on having a strong corporate culture. You must be careful with the kind of organisational culture you wish to create if you want to develop an engaging culture that will attract candidates for open positions and keep current ones. To encourage a healthy workplace culture, be on the lookout for the warning signs.

- **Do you have any fundamental values for your company?**
- **Do you remember them by heart?**
- **Do you have a workforce?**

So many businesses establish core principles because they believe they should. But after that, they do nothing productive with them. They aren't really used by the company; they only remain visible to everyone on the internet. Employee conduct is determined by a person's core values. These are definitely things you should and can do to establish a productive workplace.

What to do when you are bullied at work?

Determining what constitutes workplace bullying. Many victims of bullying find it challenging to explain their condition to others. Though it might be challenging, youngsters are aware that they are being bullied. All they can say is that talking to this individual makes them feel emotionally spent. I figured giving a good, concise description would be useful, so here it is.

Workplace bullying is a pattern of abuse that leads to a psychological power imbalance, has serious psychological and physical repercussions for the targets and their coworkers, and causes a significant financial loss to the bottom line of the firm.

The bullying is repeated first. On the other hand, if it happens once a week, it becomes bullying. Additionally, be aware that bullying frequently becomes more persistent and violent over time. Bullying is abuse, period. In fact, bullying and domestic violence are frequently contrasted by academics from throughout the world. Targets struggle to escape the vicious cycle of being in a relationship with an abuser. Bullying results in an imbalance of power in the mind. When the bully rolls his eyes or sends a nasty email, there is a first instance of hostility, but for whatever reason, the target doesn't respond. The bully continues to exhibit these behaviours over time, and the power disparity finally reaches a crescendo. By the time the target has a chance to defend herself, it is too late, and the bully has realised their power.

Getting rid of workplace bullying We are all aware that harassment at work is forbidden. But what about discrimination based on gender? - Workplace harassment is forbidden, as we all know.

What about bullying at work or equal opportunity harassment?

HR executives should be eliminating them in all the same ways for all the same reasons, even though the law regards them differently. We'll discuss how to spot workplace bullying, and I'll offer you some original solutions.

Bullying at work versus harassment at work. Let's examine a case of bullying conduct to better grasp what it entails. The three behavioural categories of aggression, humiliation, and manipulation encompass every form of bullying you can imagine. The easiest to identify is aggressive conduct. Yelling, furious outbursts, rude emails, invading someone's personal space, and making insulting statements are a few examples. Any message that we can all identify as being hostile can be cited. Let's examine the second group, humiliation. Examples include cc'ing other people on unfavourable emails, isolating someone, talking about faults in public, and spreading rumours or gossip.

Bullying has very real repercussions. There is an overwhelming amount of evidence from all around the world that shows that bullied individuals and those who witness bullying feel anxiety, stress, sadness, and even PTSD. Of course, stress contributes to a number of medical issues, including headaches and potentially heart disease.

The organisation will pay a price for all of this. Bullying diverts people, which lowers productivity and quality while increasing turnover. As a result of the distance between customers and employees and the lack of engagement and loyalty among staff members, customer service suffers. I hope that after reading this, you have a good understanding of what workplace bullying is and how it may affect both employees and those outside of a business.

So, how can bullying actions manifest themselves?

They may be divided into three groups: manipulation, humiliation, and communication. Aggressive communication includes insulting others, yelling, sending angry emails, criticising, and more. It may also be used to describe body language.

For instance, one of the guys I mentored had a reputation for speaking out at staff meetings in order to intimidate others who didn't agree with him. His body stiffened, his arms were drawn back, and his eyes appeared to be bulging out of his skull, according to the people I spoke with. When combined with his ranting, anyone who disagreed with him was quickly silenced and left feeling terrified. Humiliation includes publicly pointing out flaws, spreading rumors, mocking someone online, and other behaviors.

Another individual I tutored had a reputation for telling people they were incorrect and providing an explanation. He'd then start a 30-minute lecture on why this person's proposal was so ridiculous. He would occasionally raise his feet off the table and recline back, as if to indicate that you should settle in because explaining your idiocy would take some time. Of course this is terrible, but doing it in front of others made the poor victim feel humiliated and ashamed, and it made everyone else in the room feel quite uneasy. One business I trained for had a hazing issue. When new employees arrived, their tools would go missing, making it impossible for them to fulfil their jobs on schedule. These new employees were obviously humiliated and embarrassed, and many of them didn't leave until a few months later.

Finally, since it is so passive-aggressive, manipulation is the most difficult to spot. One woman told me she had twice the workload of everyone else in her department.

She constantly complained to her management that she couldn't keep up with the workload, but her manager assured that it wouldn't change. Then, according to her performance review, it was suggested that she be demoted since she was unable to keep up with the demands of her job. It might not have been bullying if the manager had given this lady the tools she needed to succeed, such as resources, training, or a more equitable workload distribution. The notion that she had been set up to fail stung. These stories definitely strike a chord with you if you are the victim of bullying. Try to place the actions you have encountered into one of these three categories. You may even place a star next to the sentences that really hit home with you. This is the first step you should take to ensure that others can comprehend what you're going through.

I just read a piece about the paradox of bullying at work. Although being harassed at work is an extremely distressing experience, targets are usually given very sensible guidance. In other words, I'm going to urge you to act logically and rationally from a place that seems completely irrational and illogical. It can be difficult to comprehend, but there are certain very logical procedures you must follow in order to navigate bullying securely. The most essential thing is to maintain your sense of self-worth and confidence. I am aware that the individual you work with is causing you great pain. It's critical that you take all action possible to undo the damage. Try visualising first.

Visualisation is a crucial technique for triggering your creative subconscious, which can help you come up with original solutions to get through this. Additionally, it trains your brain to notice and sense the resources you need more quickly, and it increases your internal drive to take the necessary steps to address this problem and, eventually, live a better life. Simply sit in a comfortable posture, close your eyes, and visualise working in a pleasant, healthy environment where you are valued. Do this both when you wake up and shortly before bed. Your current workplace or a new one might be involved. Try to concentrate on the feelings you are experiencing while in this unfamiliar environment. Keep such feelings close to your heart the entire day by carrying them with you. Attempt to utilise affirmations of success as well. Our thoughts and behaviours may be drastically changed through affirmations.

Stand in front of a mirror just before you go to work and tell yourself, "I am fantastic." "I am terrific." Close your office door or go outside and repeat your affirmations, "I am brave," "I'm in charge," and "I deserve respect," even if you are at work. The more you express it, the more you feel it. The more you feel, the more you believe. Your courage grows stronger the more you believe it. The more courageous you become, the closer you are to conquering bullying.

Try to also remind yourself of your successes. Every day, make a list of everything you accomplished or for which you are grateful. Writing down three positive things at the end of each day truly considerably boosts your confidence and sense of happiness with life, according to several studies conducted by positive psychologists. Setting and then achieving goals is another approach to increasing confidence.

Try participating in a marathon, signing up for a charity event, or finally enrolling in that painting class you've been wanting to take. In either case, we can be certain that individuals who establish goals, accomplish them, and then set new, also accomplishable objectives have higher levels of self-esteem than those who don't. If you want to defend your self-esteem from bullies, you must join this movement.

Try working out while we're talking about marathons. You may alleviate some of that tension and worry by exercising, which also causes the brain to create endorphins, or happy chemicals. You can fall asleep more soundly after exercising, which I know you're probably losing due to your workplace circumstances. You can also consider getting involved in activities that benefit the world. You can work together with a volunteer team to construct a house, distribute food at a food bank, or pick up trash from the beach. These successes will increase your endorphin levels, and you'll find a group of individuals who will accept you and feed your confidence. A fantastic way to feel good is to give back to your community. These actions may appear simple at first. They might not seem important to assisting you in successfully navigating bullying. They are not, I can guarantee you. Start setting aside time to partake in these pursuits, and your life will change.

Since I have experience with workplace bullying, I can assure you that those that bully do so because they are able to. Nobody warns them about it. If you are the one who tells them not to, your life will be drastically altered. People who bully do it because they are emotionally and socially insensitive. They will pay attention if you point them in the appropriate direction on how to treat you. They may even respect you, I observe.

So, here are some pointers for accomplishing that. Use the person's name as much as you can. Perhaps it sounds like this: I'm not here to dispute Rick . Rick I just want you to quit screaming. Rick I respect you, and I demand the same respect in return. Rick please stop shouting from now on. I'm sorry if it sounds odd, but picture a dad who calls his troubled child by his whole name. You're going to indicate authority over this individual at work, just as it implies dominance over the youngster.

Employ your language. You've probably heard that using the I language is the best way to express your emotions. We're frequently told to use the phrase, "I feel horrible when you do this." But when it comes to bullying, change it up. Try using the phrase "you need to focus on treating people more professionally, Juan," rather than "I don't like the way you treat me." Juan is now responsible for his own conduct as a result.

Additionally, try using questions to deflect criticism. The power is with the one who asks questions. As a result, your conversation may sound like this. - You keep making errors in this report. Just repeatedly, and always in error. You have to show how stupid you are to someone else in this area. You can't be the only one who thinks you're a moron, right?- Could you specify exactly what went wrong? I have no time to train moron. You ought to be proficient in doing your duties. Again, what specifically can I change? To begin with, you computed the figures on page three incorrectly. Do I need to use a different formula? I make use of the same one as everyone else.

You see what I mean. You put the onus on them to make clear what the genuine problem is. In order to address the issue and move on, you've requested useful information. Another tool to try is fogging. It implies that you deflect criticism by endorsing it. This is advantageous since it will surprise the critic. Here is one instance. The concepts you brought forth in our meeting this morning were thus absurd. You know, initially, many despised Steve Jobs' concepts as being really foolish, and now look where he is. The target is evidently not affected by the criticism.

When are you leaving this place and starting a new job? Everyone here abhors having to work with you. - I mean, having every single employee here despise me has to be a record. I understand that at first this may seem difficult, but with some practise at home and if you get the feel of it, it can actually be entertaining. It resembles a contest of wits. To be clear, this is only one way to defend oneself. You could think it comes out as a little passive aggressive. I don't advocate becoming passive aggressive, but I do advocate for self-defense.

Always behave honourably. Follow your gut instinct. The last piece of advice I have for you is to speak assertively rather than passively. The capacity to use free, non-defensive expression of your thoughts and feelings is known as assertive language. People who are assertive can articulate their demands and goals in a style that is convincing and professional. Compare this strong remark to its more passive counterpart. Instead of hoping we can all get along, it's crucial that we respect one another so that we can work as a team. See how using passive language suggests that you are unsure of yourself and what you are saying? I'm hoping is vague and not really clear.

Additionally, attempt assertiveness in its three phases. They are problem, solution, and validation. Validation demonstrates that you are aware of the other person. It merely means you're trying to understand their perspective, not that you agree with them. Empathy makes it easier for others to listen to what you have to say next. Explaining why something has to change is referred to be a problem. A precise request for a specific change in behaviour is provided by the solution.

Be mindful of your body language. 93% of communication is nonverbal, as you are surely aware. Even if the often cited statistic is untrue, it serves as a useful reminder of the significance of nonverbal communication. Your mouth is the sole place where words may be expressed. Nonverbal cues include your posture, eye contact, gestures, facial expressions, physical attributes like height and weight, clothing, jewellery, and even the way you smell. They also include your voice tone, pitch, loudness, and other vocal characteristics.

While words are crucial, there is also a lot of nonverbal communication that we need to pay attention to while interacting with others. Because of this, we tend to trust nonverbal cues from people more than spoken ones. If I tell my boss that I enjoy working for him but I frequently arrive late and don't contribute much, he could conclude that I don't. He will place more weight on the tardiness and lack of output than the words. And your bully will trust your nonverbal language if you want them to think they can't treat you badly but you hunch your shoulders. Thankfully, we have the ability to regulate our nonverbal cues, and the first step in doing so is to become hyperaware of it. I want you to start doing this right away. Consider what your body is doing at this very now with your body.

- **Do you have your back to your laptop?**
- **Your hands and arms are where?**

You should now lean back in your chair, elevate your chin, place your hands on your knees, and place both of your feet firmly on the floor. To finish this course, continue to sit in that position. Because you're sitting in that position, your brain is currently creating testosterone. This substance is responsible for confidence and aggressiveness. When communicating with a bully, you'll need this crucial tool. Our self-assured body language not only communicates to your brain that you want testosterone, but it also conveys to those around you that you are in fact self-assured. Standing or sitting straight up, pointing your toes squarely in the direction of the other person you are speaking with, keeping your hands at your sides or on your hips, and making eye contact are all examples of confident nonverbal communication. When speaking to someone, look them in the eyes directly. This is more effective than standing unconfidently with your legs crossed, head bowed, shoulders shrugged, and arms crossed.

Keep in mind that paralanguage, or anything in your voice other than your words, also counts as nonverbal communication. For instance, our speech tone reveals to our listeners whether we are excited or bored. Most people interpret a rapid pace as anxiousness. In order to sound more aggressive, try the following. Avoid talking over others and always end a sentence with a question. By doing that, you are implying that you are looking for approval. Make sure to conclude with a period instead. Slow down your speech. Speaking quickly usually conveys that you are anxious. Discard filler; phrases like "this is just my opinion" or "uh" suggest you are unsure of yourself. Be at ease in the stillness.

Most individuals find silence to be unsettling. You therefore hold the apex of the discussion if you are at ease with situations like when you pose a question and don't immediately receive a response. The following time a bully approaches, concentrate on your combat stance: keep your head held high, lean slightly forward with your toes pointing forward, place your hands on your hips or by your side, and make solid, extended eye contact. By doing this, you can deal with hostile coworkers without saying a word.

Make sure they are first mentioned in your monthly or quarterly check-ins, on your forms, and in your performance management system. Then you can gauge a person's level of commitment to the key principles. Your basic beliefs undoubtedly don't allow for bullying, so anyone indulging in that conduct would be dealt with.

Make sure your interview process incorporates your fundamental principles. Values-related behavioural interview questions should be asked. and discover what your guiding principles mean to them.

Integrate key principles into the culture at large. Choose one day every month and plan activities for it. Create a programme in which people can nominate one another for upholding basic principles. Ensure that everyone has a pleasant and vibrant frame displaying the fundamental principles on their workstation. and make sure they are brought up at each meeting. As the HR representative or manager, evaluate your own procedures to determine if they align with the core principles and make any required adjustments.

- **Do you leave for home at a respectable time if work-life balance is a fundamental value?**
- **How precisely does it manifest itself in your team?**
- **Do you regard each and every individual that enters your workplace like a client if providing excellent customer service is one of your key values?**
- **Do you give them a warm welcome? Do you give them your undivided attention?**
- **How does your group embody each of its tenets?**

- **Are there any places where the team might demonstrate them more effectively?**

Have a meeting with your staff to go through the same. Lastly, provide people the tools they need to halt bad conduct by applying the basic principles. Empower them to state that one of our key beliefs is customer service, and that comment seemed like something you would not say to a client if they observed or encountered any unpleasant activity. Or perhaps innovation is one of our guiding principles. Even though this was certainly not your intention, your email seemed to discourage cooperation and the exchange of ideas. You must genuinely make your workers feel supported in avoiding bullying and harassment through one-on-one conversations, staff meetings, and emails if you want to stop it.

How many of you believe that training on the subject of workplace bullying is a wonderful method to put an end to harassment? I concur. Each employee should be aware of what it is, how it appears, and what your policy is against participating in it. But I also advise training that emphasises productive work habits—the actions you actually want. Trainings on conflict resolution, interpersonal communication, internal customer service, and other topics may significantly impact bullying prevention and cultural change. The Equal Employment Opportunity Commission also suggests civility training and bystander training. Keep in mind that the effectiveness of any training depends on the implementation of the lessons learned. If participants receive training on how to give constructive criticism, make sure it's happening by checking in with everyone and rewarding those who do it effectively.

Additional training on bullying is required for managers, and this training should cover how to establish standards with staff members, coach bullies, handle complaints, and foster a constructive work environment within their own teams. Additionally, management by moving about and managerial communication techniques have to be covered. Additionally, managers require instruction on how to conduct performance-related dialogues with staff members because these interactions might occasionally be seen as bullying.

An employee will claim that the talks are harsh and seem like assaults, while a manager may claim that she is only keeping someone accountable. Managers should take on the role of a performance coach if they have established clear standards and an employee isn't living up to them. This will lessen any sense of bullying. Employees won't feel attacked if they believe their boss is collaborating with them to get better, supporting them while they do so, and offering encouragement along the way.

Of course, if the employee isn't meeting standards despite all of this, the manager will have a disciplinary dialogue. I also advise managers to be held responsible for creating a supportive workplace. If you're doing any kind of climate survey, for instance, you may examine the climate inside each team and identify the areas that need improvement. Create zany presentations, think of amusing activities, and get employees enthused about a more positive workplace. After all, the goal of these training sessions is to create a good environment.

According to the climate evaluation, 30% of the organisation had experienced harassment, and some people were unhappy. What led to this? I can only assume that those who were satisfied with their lives completed the climate survey, and those who were dissatisfied completed the engagement survey. The moral of the story is that while my climate assessment was longer and provided a deep understanding of relationships, satisfaction, engagement, harassment, and bullying, as well as whether certain demographics feel differently than others, their engagement survey measured enthusiasm with few questions, and the positive scores had them thinking their organisation was doing just fine.

I'm advocating that in order to modify behaviour, you must first make an effort to comprehend it. If you want to handle it internally, you can select questions from a tonne of surveys online, but if you don't have much expertise doing surveys, I suggest hiring a professional. The wording of the poll and many other details are crucial to its validity. Surveys have the key benefits of being completely anonymous, which encourages individuals to express their opinions honestly, and having quantitative findings, which allow you to benchmark and track progress the next time you conduct the survey.

People should be rated on factors such as their comfort level in reporting harassment or bullying to their supervisors, their level of confidence in their team and manager, and whether or not their company inspires them to perform at their best every single day. Also, provide lots of opportunities for individuals to reply with open-ended inquiries. Regarding comments, we also interview a 10% random sample of the workforce when we undertake climate surveys. The chance to pose incisive inquiries is priceless. People will be far more honest with a stranger who doesn't know them and can't take action against them; thus, I also recommend an outsider for this.

HR is thought to control the livelihoods of its employees. Because the information from interviews is sometimes somewhat random, it can be challenging to evaluate, but my team and I will search for trends and organise our notes accordingly. The knowledge is easier to understand and put to use because of the topics. My main piece of advice is to make sure you're going to act on the results as soon as possible following the survey, whether you conduct it internally or hire a professional. Inaction will result in you betraying trust. It will give the impression that you took the results seriously if you present a list of three to five steps you'll take right now to improve the environment.

Additionally, provide your staff with a summary report so they are aware that nothing was kept a secret. If individuals are unhappy, survey findings could be a little discouraging, but you can't address it if you don't know about it. Inhale deeply, then plunge in.

The key factor influencing workplace bullying in a company is whether or not its leaders allow it.

I'm not implying that your leaders aim to foster a culture of bullying. They are most likely unaware of it, don't believe it's a big concern, or downplay the harm it is doing. But it's crucial that leaders convey the right message about creating a pleasant workplace. They need to make it known how important a positive culture is and how they will hold individuals accountable.

Leaders must also set an example for the actions they wish to see in others. They should refrain from promoting those who don't adhere to your company's basic principles and explicitly commend those who do. You may still affect behaviour even if you're not the CEO, especially if you work in human resources or are a manager or supervisor. Make it clear that you won't put up with harassment within your own team or department at work. People who exhibit the proper conduct should be rewarded, and those who don't should be disciplined in conjunction with HR.

You may influence the behaviour of your employees using your performance management system.

Inform negative people that their actions don't suit the culture of your team and that they should change. Depending on your personality and background, I realise it could seem frightening, but your company has given you the authority to address organisational issues. They depend on you to control the actions and output of your team. Also bear in mind that by tolerating terrible conduct, you are essentially saying that bad behaviour is okay. Because they know you won't take action, employees won't report any more improper actions to you. I'm sorry to say it, but your lack of trust will prevent you from managing people very well. just some ideas to ponder.

You may already have a policy against bullying, and you undoubtedly have one against harassment. Why not have a policy that outlines what is expected or a "Healthy Workplace Policy" instead of all these regulations being about what is forbidden? So, this is how you make it. First, divide participants into groups of four at your next staff meeting and allow them 15 minutes to respond to this one question.

How do you want your peers and bosses to treat you? If your company is too large or too dispersed to hold company-wide meetings, delegate this exercise to department heads to complete in their own teams. Ask each group to report its findings after 15 minutes. Write them down on paper that is displayed on a screen as they are called out so that everyone can see what is being said. Surprisingly, the majority of groups will provide the same 15 or so responses. Employees will come to understand that they want to be treated equally to everyone else at work. You now have a fantastic list of actions to include in your healthy workplace policy.

Next, return to your workstation and organise comparable objects into groups or search for topics. I frequently simply begin classifying things as I see them. After that, insert bullet points into the appropriate categories. You could observe a pattern of bullet points that use the words acknowledge, applaud, give thanks, and appreciate others' good work, for instance. All of the points can be grouped under the heading "appreciation." Perhaps there are bullets like, "Listen, speak in a polite manner, and share knowledge with anybody who needs it." Now you have a topic or category called professional or successful communication. Create a list of behaviours for your healthy workplace policy by combining your themes.

When you distribute the new policy, remind everyone that the list of behaviours came from the exercise and express your gratitude for their assistance. In the exercise files, I offer a sample of a healthy workplace policy. Before putting it into practise, make sure to have your employment law attorney review it. And always keep in mind that it's a great exercise to concentrate on what you want from employees rather than what you don't.

Harassment and bullying at work do not occur in a vacuum. They take place inside the framework of your company. As a result, when bullying or harassment occurs, it is because the organisation allowed it to happen.

Uncertain tasks and responsibilities, a workforce comprised of long-term workers, highly intellectual personnel like attorneys or engineers, bureaucracy and rule-oriented cultures, and the lack of disciplinary action for earlier offenders are all contributing factors. Again, bullying is more probable if one or more of these risk factors are present. If avoiding harassment and bullying is genuinely a goal, there is a lot to be done. I advise discussing these risk factors and working out how to get rid of them with your organisation's executives. To determine if compensation is equal, you may, for instance, conduct a pay audit. Make sure you provide your employees with a work-life balance and some breathing room despite the pressure and crazily tight deadlines. Or consider if the numerous rules and regulations that make you appear bureaucratic are actually required.

Every employee in your company has a right to be respected at work. Additionally, everyone is entitled to establish appropriate boundaries. Your responsibility as an HR professional, manager, or supervisor is to assist in establishing these limits. You must immediately report any instances of rudeness, bullying, or harassment if you witness them. You are encouraging the conduct if you don't. Your continued silence implies approval. Here are three actions to take in the heat of the moment. Validate.

Express your understanding of their feelings. Describe the issue. Describe the undesirable conduct and the reasons it is ineffective. Use detailed examples and be extremely explicit. Don't speak in generalities. Provide a resolution. Give advice on what this individual should do in its place. Here is an illustration of how to apply these procedures. Avoid displaying emotion. Stay composed and firm. Stay assured. Although it may look a little frightening, this actually works. If your toes are pointing forward, your chin is up, and your shoulders are back, your body language might make you feel strong. Make direct eye contact as well. Several times, use the person's name. When you address someone by their name, they are more likely to pay attention and realise you are talking to them specifically. It is not filler. Last but not least, I do urge you to tell it right away, especially in front of others.

As a coach who specialises in working with bullies, I can't divulge all of my secrets, but I can give you some insight into how it works. I am aware of several instances where a manager or HR specialist actually made significant advancements and changed behaviour. I thus hope you'll give it a shot. Getting some intelligence is the first step. This individual lacks social and emotional intelligence, therefore they have no idea how their actions are affecting others. They will be much more successful in enacting change if they are aware of how they are truly seen and the implications this has on their own efficacy. Get the consent of your coachee before letting them know that a 360-degree assessment is the ideal place to start. You might even ask them to provide you with the names of potential interview subjects. You will enquire about the communication style of your coachee as well as about his or her strengths and shortcomings. It goes without saying that you will inform the interviewers as to why your coachee is coaching, but you won't explain it to them.

Second, identify themes in the outcomes to make the data more palatable. t's useless to have a big list of bullet points in a haphazard sequence. Rearrange and group your interview notes according to topics to improve confidentiality. Make sure the identity of the speaker is obscure.

Third, talk to your coachee about the 360 feedback. Only explain the outcomes at that meeting and leave time for their response as this is a moment of truth sort of meeting. Delete any more coaching material. Just focus on reading the findings.

Fourth, you'll check up with your coachee a few days later to see how they're doing. The majority of the time, I discover that the person has done some soul-searching and acknowledges that at least part of the criticism is accurate. The beginning is excellent.

Your coaching will then focus on assisting the person in learning the reasons behind their current views and the methods they may use to alter them. Choose a theme from your 360, talk about why it exists, and then brainstorm ways to change it at least once every week. As relationships are formed, the coachee will eventually discover that making these adjustments is improving his or her life. And at that point, you can be sure the changes will last. I always reinterview folks at some point over the course of my coaching, which often lasts for four to six months, to find out what developments other participants are seeing. I must conclude with a warning: if you're internal, people might not be completely honest with you. Since outside consultants and coaches are strangers, people could see them as being more trustworthy because nothing negative can be said about them or recorded in their personnel file. In any event, read my book on coaching to find out more about the coaching procedure and the reasons why individuals bully others.

Many of my coworkers refer to employees who are aware of or observe bullying as bystanders or witnesses. We frequently see such phrases online as well, although I prefer the term reinforcer. I'll explain why I think that is a better description. Bystander and witness are passive nouns; you may both observe and be a bystander in a vehicle accident, but you can't do anything to stop it. You won't leap in between the two vehicles to prevent a collision, I assure you.

However, you may intervene at work. Additionally, each day that you consciously choose not to, you are demonstrating that the behaviour will be accepted. By giving the conduct your tacit approval by remaining silent, you are encouraging it. Bullying never takes place in a vacuum. It's not just about those two individuals; it's a societal phenomena, and if it's occurring in your place of employment, you're a part of it. Now I see why folks consciously choose not to walk in every day; it's terrifying. They worry about being punished and wonder if the leaders would defend them. They also worry about their livelihood. But if you work in human resources or are a manager or supervisor, you can halt this conduct. The decision to support a peaceful and productive workplace must be made by each individual as well as by you.

Recognise that everyone who brings you a complaint of any kind is doing so out of trust and because they need your assistance. It's not an easy choice for them to share their stories with you. This person is asking for your help and direction. Your initial meeting's objective is to comprehend this person's perspective and to show empathy. But use caution before reacting too strongly. The complainant will assume that you have taken their side if you reply, "I can't believe that occurred," but it's too early to do that.

Additionally, watch out for passing judgement or making any assumptions while you're listening. Take notes, ask probing questions, and pay close attention to all this individual has to say while being completely impartial. Make eye contact with the person and use open body language. Make eye contact with your employee and smile to show that you are interested in what they have to say. Finally, if appropriate, provide advice. Give the individual complaining some advice on how to deal with those behaviours if you hear them reporting that someone routinely screams or sends scathing letters. You might suggest that the subsequent abusive email be answered with the simple message "I will no longer respond to emails like these." I'd be pleased to react if you'd want to reword this in a more formal tone. Don't forget to let them know you'll back them in their efforts to speak out for themselves. A warning, please. Giving advice is challenging. Too frequently, when someone feels mistreated, the only advise given is to try to resolve the issue with the other party.

Avoid going there right away since it might be difficult for someone who feels abused to work things out. Please do so if they urge you to intervene and assist them. That might entail involving HR, speaking with the other person to learn about their perspective, acting as a mediator, or relocating one or both of them to separate them. Just make sure you don't leave them hanging and don't think the problem will go away once you've given them some advice and a solution. Continue to check in on the complainant to make sure they're alright, and of course, if it's a complaint of discrimination or harassment, you must adhere to company regulations on that.

Do you penalise those that arrive late a lot or maybe terminate them?

What about those who routinely fail to achieve deadlines or quotas? Employers frequently punish employees for these actions, and you may do the same for bullying. Bullying is a performance issue, plain and simple. And the quicker you get involved, the simpler it is to fix. In order to have a productive talk about altering bullying behaviour, follow these steps. First, by giving succinct and clear examples, assist the person in understanding that they are regarded as being excessively aggressive. Even if you weren't there when the behaviour occurred, you may still point to the numerous complaints you've received.

You'll get much further in boosting people's performance if you approach them with politeness and make inquiries like, "I noticed your reports haven't been as complete as we need. Is there anything going on I can help you with?" Remember that criticising or calling out errors in front of others will almost certainly cause them to perform worse because they will be scared and distracted by your criticism. The next stage is to hopefully feel prepared to discontinue destructive conduct at work. A triple victory is bullying's elimination. Bullies communicate more effectively once their behaviour has been corrected. Due to the team's lack of fear, they are more productive. And since it is a safer and more inclusive workplace, the business is more effective.

Last but not least, make sure your organisation has a good policy that forbids bullying and demands professionalism, and then hold individuals responsible for following it. Make sure your performance management system includes fundamental principles and that individuals are also held responsible for them. Distrust in leaders and their willingness to treat these problems seriously is the main risk factor that has to be eliminated. Make sure the staff is aware that harassment and bullying are strictly prohibited.

According to Benjamin Franklin, "you are planning to fail by failing to prepare." And the same is true when visiting HR to discuss bullying; thus, here are a few things I advise doing. You should first handle any negative performance reviews your abusive manager may have given you. Positive and continual appraisals of performance are effective. They provide you precise goals to accomplish and helpful criticism. If your review doesn't fit that description and your boss is also shouting at you, humiliating you, and claiming credit for your job, bullying may be going place. But we need more information. Send your employer an email asking for a meeting to go through your evaluation. Send a couple more if your request is not heeded. You can demonstrate to HR that you sought to gather information but were unsuccessful if your manager doesn't answer. If your request is granted, make sure to go through in your meeting the precise behaviours that must be improved, your particular objectives and timetables, and the criteria by which your success will be judged.

Second, make an effort to stop the bullying on your own. Consider this. Prior to complaining, a target who has taken action to address their own problems has a stronger case. Choose the scenario that, if you were in HR, you would choose from the ones below by giving them some thought. I need to chat to you, so hello. I need your assistance since my manager and I are not getting along. Sure, what's happening? - Rick is being unfair to me. He's simply incredibly disrespectful, as seen by the way he rudely interrupted me at yesterday's staff meeting.

Additionally, he gave me a terrible performance review this quarter, even though past managers have usually given me excellent reviews, so I'm not sure what's going on there. - Have you discussed this with Rick? No, not really. I haven't been able to talk to him since he makes me so anxious. - Yeah. We'll investigate. Hey. - I have to speak with you for a little while. I need your assistance since my manager and I are not getting along. - Yes, what's happening? - Rick is being unfair to me. He's simply incredibly disrespectful, as seen by the way he rudely interrupted me at yesterday's staff meeting. And this quarter, he gave me a terrible employee assessment. I've always had excellent reviews, so I'm not sure why this is. Have you discussed this with Rick? - I have, indeed. After the staff meeting, I informed him that I thought he was treating me disrespectfully, and he responded by saying that I was being overly sensitive. I've written emails to him over the last two weeks asking for a meeting to discuss my performance assessment, but he has never replied. A copy of the four emails I sent is provided below. If he won't offer me comments and tell me what to do differently, I can't get better. I've attempted to talk to Rick about his conduct but he won't talk to me, so I'm going to you. I have some suggestions on what I can do, Okay.

I have a few ideas on what I can do, but before I do anything, I wanted to hear your thoughts. - I'm delighted you came, though. I'd be delighted to assist. Anyone would choose option B. Unlike the person in scenario A, who seems powerless and unable to cooperate with others, this individual exudes confidence and the ability to handle their own difficulties. Determine the organisation's costs third. You must ascertain how much money the bully is costing since HR and leaders understand the business language of money. Have you ever heard him shout at patrons? Has her actions caused anyone to resign? Fourth, get knowledgeable. Are you facing harassment, discrimination, bullying, or workplace violence as a result of this behaviour? You must be familiar with the appropriate jargon. Do some internet study to learn the lingo of HR. Fifth, make sure you are clear about your expectations of HR before speaking with them. What are your objectives and anticipated results? Do you want HR to act or are you just looking to spread information? What sort of response are you anticipating? Additionally, think about what you'll do if the talk doesn't result in what you desire. Make some introspection.

"Don't let toxic people infect you with the fear of giving and receiving one of the most powerful forces in this world... Love!"

You demonstrate that it's okay for everyone else to stand up for themselves by doing this. It demonstrates your concern for their well-being and your will to reject negativity. When the time comes, you'll be prepared to defend a fruitful and positive workplace culture. I'm referring to organisational risk factors, or those that might allow for undesirable conduct to occur, as discovered by researchers that examine unfavourable work environments. Risk factors for harassment include unequal remuneration, the failure to punish past offenders, social networks that exclude particular groups, and a lack of confidence in reporting to HR and supervisors, among other things.

Harassment is more likely to occur if one or more of these risk factors are present. This interests me since training programmes are frequently used by businesses to avoid harassment, but if these risk factors are present, they are of little benefit in that regard. Risk factors for workplace bullying include demanding circumstances like unreasonable deadlines, overwhelming workloads, internal competitiveness, or rapid change.

How will you identify a toxic work environment?

Do you work for a business with a toxic workplace?

Before accepting the job offer, look out for these subtly telling symptoms of a hostile work environment. When you work in toxic environments, you suffer in both your personal and professional lives. Here are telltale indications of a hazardous workplace, along with advice on how to avoid (or leave) them. Everybody experiences awful Mondays, trying weeks, and even depressing months. That is how a career cycles.

It takes more than merely "hating" your job to create a poisonous workplace. However, you can usually get through a tough Monday, make it through a difficult week, and take something positive away from a poor quarter. The equivalent of experiencing each of these difficulties again without a break is a toxic work environment. Red flags are piled on top of each other. It's a manager who uses passive aggression or insensitive remarks made by your employees about the guy you replaced. It has fewer borders (or none at all). It uses mansplaining, gaslighting, and microaggressions, and it's toxic as all get out. These are the top (or worse) signs of a poisonous society, in your opinion. One of these may be harmful, but it could also be fixable if your workplace has one. Skip the hazmat suit and start looking for a new job if your workplace exhibits some of these signs, if not all of them.

As there are no core values, thus unwanted subcultures will emerge and threaten the success of your company. Lack of corporate fundamental principles is arguably the most alarming indicator of a terrible company culture. These serve as an organisation's driving force; if you lack fundamental values, your culture is more likely to develop aimlessly.

Where managers do not apply their essential values. The issue is that workers turn to supervisors for guidance. Employees will follow senior and middle management's example if they don't uphold the key principles you've established. Even worse, they'll start to doubt management since they let managers get away with breaking the rules. There will be a distinct separation between the leadership and the employees, and authority will lose its credibility. If it's not proper in the workplace and wasn't cool in middle school. Gossip breeds unwelcome cliques that alienate your team, pitting workers against one another and fostering a climate of mistrust.

You either end up participating in or being the victim of office gossip. Negative workplace conversations have a negative impact on peer relationships and teamwork, which leads to hostile conduct. Whatever your stance, engaging in gossip will only sour the working environment.

A toxic workplace culture is almost always characterised by high employee turnover.A negative company culture will not only turn away employees, but it will also discourage potential hires from considering your company seriously. More than 30% of employees claim they quit their jobs within the first 90 days because the "company culture was not as expected," and 20% said they switched industries as a result of a "toxic work environment or culture." A negative company culture will not only turn away current employees but will also discourage potential ones from considering your company seriously. If you're losing workers left and right, they're definitely seeking a workplace with a less hazardous environment.

Communication issues may be present in a toxic workplace. Poor communication is a surefire sign of a hazardous workplace environment. The way information flows between teams or between managers and direct reports may have an effect on both the company's culture and its financial performance. Ineffective communication among staff members can reduce productivity, hinder innovation, and foster an unfavourable work atmosphere. So many issues at work are caused by inadequate, unclear, or disorganised communication.

In actuality, effective communication is one of the most crucial abilities for every successful firm. Why? The term "communication" covers a wide range of topics, including listening abilities (both as a manager and an employee), verbal and written communication, communication preferences, and much more. So how can you detect whether poor communication is causing toxicity at work? A major problem is the general lack of communication. Other issues include the ongoing lack of project clarity and the inconsistent messages sent to various staff. Communication that is passively antagonistic, has poor listening skills, and is frequently "off hours". Bad organisations—or excellent organisations performing poorly—have communication issues at their core. Employees who receive poor communication frequently become confused and feel purposeless. From this point on, issues develop and exacerbate, frequently resulting in everything else on our list.

You know that a healthy competition benefits businesses. As there is a lot of competitive pressure. It inspires personnel and promotes exceptional performance, which can aid in the expansion of your business. However, making competition the centre of your culture will lead to hatred among your workforce.

Where employees frequently arrive late or miss work leads to high rates of absenteeism or excessive tardiness are blatant indicators of a toxic workplace culture. A company employee's tardiness should indicate to you that they are either unmotivated or lazy, which is a bad characteristic that will harm your culture. Employees that regularly miss work are also usually unmotivated and uninterested in their jobs, with remote or flexible schedule employees being the exception.

If workers frequently work through lunch, it's either because they feel they don't have enough time to take a break or because they think management doesn't support doing so. More than three-quarters of employees believe that lunch breaks increase job performance, so not only is this bad business reasoning, but it's also a certain way to turn away potential employees. It is absurd to expect workers to do quality work after eight straight hours of constant labour. Additionally, it sends a message to them that leadership does not respect their personal devotion to the business or contribution to the culture—only their job output.

The business does not support the community. If your company doesn't offer a matching programme for charitable contributions, doesn't provide an annual day of service for community service, or never issues requests for donations following a devastating hurricane or other disaster, you're sending the message that you don't give a damn about the outside world.

A toxic workplace may have poor communication; it may have cliques, exclusion, and gossipy behaviour; it may have poor leadership; it probably has unmotivated employees; it may have stunted growth. A toxic workplace frequently lacks work-life balance and has a high employee turnover rate.

Gut feelings are triggered by a toxic workplace. Unhealthy workplaces encourage conflict, rivalry, low morale, ongoing stress, negativity, illness, high turnover, and even bullying. What's worse? Toxic workplaces are rarely retained. They frequently follow you inside. They dominate your interactions with family members, rob you of much-needed sleep, and overall raise your anxiety and stress levels.

Where employees leave negative comments about the company. Not offereing any platforms for anonymous reviews have made any company's culture more visible. Positivity at work and highly engaged staff members only strengthen your appeal to potential applicants. However, job searchers will find out first, harming your company's reputation, if your workforce is dissatisfied with the management approach, experiencing fierce peer rivalry, or having a demoralizingly high turnover rate.

Where employees are not accepted or paid. Your culture suffers if you simply acknowledge the top sales representative each quarter. The majority of the workforce will feel underpaid and disrespected if rewards are only infrequently given to a select few people. It may also result in a toxic workplace culture built on rivalry and hostility among coworkers.

Where managers seldom make internal promotions. If all of your new recruits come from outside the organisation, particularly at the management and leadership levels, you're conveying the wrong message that current employees are either unimportant or unqualified for advancement. Both statements impede progress by fostering a hostile workplace atmosphere.

Managers speak out in public about employees. Employees occasionally make poor mistakes. When employees commit mistakes, a toxic work environment calls them out by name and highlights them in public forums.

Individuals often work late or on weekends if your team's average daily attendance exceeds the 5-hour mark on a regular basis, it might raise some red flags. This indicates that either your team members are overburdened with responsibilities or that management has unrealistic expectations for their direct reports. Quotas guarantee that your growth strategy remains on course, but unrealistic goals can cause staff fatigue.

Applicants are required for culture fit while it's understandable that you want every team member to experience a sense of belonging in your business culture, recruiting for cultural fit is an outmoded approach that will lose you top talent. Your culture will stagnate or worsen if you only hire people who are exact replicas of your present staff. When it comes to pushing the envelope, like-minded people prefer to butt heads but are terrific at agreeing.

In this day and age, failing to actively and successfully recruit, attract, and retain women, gender nonconforming individuals, and people of colour, as well as to foster an inclusive workplace culture, reeks of corporate ignorance and adds to a toxic work environment. Employees get the impression that management doesn't care when there isn't a corporate giving culture, for example.

- **How do your needs—physical, emotional, or environmental—affect your creativity and productivity?**
- **What worries are keeping you from moving forward?**
- **What is your default action when you're under stress?**
- **What drives you, to your knowledge?**
- **What desires may lead you astray?**

Become comfortable talking about your own worries and anxieties while being aware of those of your colleagues. Humans' innate biological and behavioural reactions to fear are widely known. Fight, flight, and freeze in the workplace manifest as resource hoarding, project-defeating competition, and excessive deadlines established by supervisors.

According to one study, these actions are virtually always the outcome of an unspoken fear of shortage and a scarcity mindset. When employees are under stress or uncertain about their position, they tend to fall into these behaviours. When we talk freely and honestly about our worries, they are frequently reduced. To help people feel psychologically comfortable talking about their anxieties in a work environment, the leader must first disclose their own worries. Many of the poisonous behaviours that have been appearing will disappear on their own once the entire team is able to discuss fear openly.

Assist others in achieving their goals without getting in the way.However, if carried too far, any of these fundamental drivers might backfire. Too much emphasis on winning might encourage dishonest behaviour. Frustration might result from spending an excessive amount of time reading, studying, and not really accomplishing. In the correct situation, wanting to assist others is fantastic, but when one stops meeting their own needs in order to do so, it may turn into destructive people-pleasing.

People will be more motivated if you understand what they truly desire for them, but you must watch out that they don't receive too much of a good thing. Someone who craves independence may aggressively oppose or sabotage coworkers who want to work with them if you give them too much room. People readily veer into poisonous area when their needs get in the way (when they are highly competitive or always seeking approval, for example). Managers must focus on spotting the first indications of hazardous conduct. House fires are difficult to put out, whereas minor flare-ups are.

A particular toxic group of coworkers who regularly gather for lunch, coffee, and happy hours; projects frequently given to this group regardless of talent or experience; significant portions of the workday spent whispering or chatting on messaging platforms; a general outward lack of interest on the part of the group in anyone else—unless it involves gossip or "drama".

We don't mean to imply that you should base your evaluation of your job on the calibre (or lack thereof) of people around you. It will, however, have an impact on you if your job is filled with uninspired coworkers. There are two ways you could respond to uninspired employees. You'll take on a lot of the work that they're not managing and end up exhausted. Their lack of desire will frustrate you and cause you to experience under-challenged burnout. Your coworkers may exhaust you just as easily as they can inspire you to work more, be better, and nurture new ideas. Employee disengagement typically stems from a much more serious organisational issue. Perhaps there has been poor top-down communication. Disorganisation, disillusionment with the leadership, or general mistrust might be the causes. Whatever it is, if the people around you lack motivation, your workplace is poisonous.

Speaking of development, even if it's simply personally toxic for you, your job could be toxic if you're not experiencing it. Your employer is probably not interested in your professional development if they don't seem to provide any options for mentoring, mobility, or learning opportunities to advance your knowledge or career. It could be time to alter the soil if you realise you have nowhere to grow.

A hazardous workplace is very much guaranteed to have a high rate of employee turnover. It might be difficult to decide to leave a job. Something is seriously wrong when you observe that decision being made by a number of people. On the other hand, if staff members are often let go or dismissed, this may point to some other hazardous factors.

A high turnover rate typically denotes inefficiency, a lack of focus, poor leadership, or limited opportunities. Keep an eye on your company's turnover rate.

There is frequently no work-life balance in toxic workplaces. You should be able to live a complete life away from work. You ought to have the option to turn off Slack alerts. After supper on a Tuesday, you should be able to leave an email unopened. You shouldn't have to feel bad about attending your dental visit.

In this chapter, I've spoken a little bit about burnout. The term "burnout" goes beyond the vocabulary used in the workplace. The World Health Organisation recognises workplace burnout as a valid medical illness. Burnout is often a telltale symptom of toxic workplaces, or at the very least, of workplaces that don't "work" for you. These three forms of burnout are listed.

Any of these phrases ring a bell with you?

Employees who put a lot of effort into their work in the hopes of getting good results experience frenetic burnout. The frantic worker does not see results after a long time of diligent labor. Employees who are bored and underchallenged at work may experience burnout. The underchallenged personnel discover themselves in a depressed state since they are unable to find any fulfilment in their work.

An employee who has been consistently under stress at work for an extended period of time is said to be worn-out. The worn-out employee feels demoralised and uninspired by the work at hand after receiving insignificant compensation. Consider leaving your hazardous employment if you experience any of these forms of workplace burnout.

Dangerous work environments can sometimes grow from a small seed. This is when things start to go wrong, whether the cause is poor management, a disastrous economic year, or an organisational-wide failure to maintain the company's objectives. If you used to think well of your job but now find it difficult to express praise for it, you're likely dealing with a fresh form of toxicity that prevents you from moving forward. Your movement stalling or coming to a complete stop is typically an indication of a more serious issue. It's a clue that things are getting toxic if your profession isn't moving ahead, especially if it was one where you had previously experienced progress. It may be time to think about leaving your job.

If your workplace exhibits any of the aforementioned characteristics, it may even be poisonous. You might be working in a hostile environment. Workplaces that are hostile are much worse, and a lot of the inter-office conduct is probably unlawful. Consider some of these indicators of a blatantly hostile workplace.

Do you believe that working from home "doesn't happen" toxicity?

68% of workers who work from home still experience major burnout, according to a new Monster.com study on remote work burnout. Why? Well, to put it briefly, it's because some of us never actually switch off. Workplace burnout is a likely outcome when work-related pressures are combined with those from the home, childcare, the partner working in a totally different field nearby, and the transformation of your house into a working environment that is open 24/7. Imagine for a moment that burnout is a problem for the entire crew. Your marketing associate's tardy email now looks to be a personal slight. Do they not realise how busy you are? What a slight!

A once-healthy workplace can suddenly become poisonous due to worker fatigue. By arranging 1:1 meetings, relaxation, really encouraging self-care, and putting "pleasure" into your work weeks, you may fight this.The secret to successful digital cooperation is effective communication. Find opportunities for your team to simulate water cooler time, connect, and detach from work so that you can periodically calibrate. Buzzing workplaces raise the possibility of a harmful workplace atmosphere once more.

The hallways of the workplace are once more crowded with employees. However, the potential of a negative workplace culture has grown as a result of the higher attendance.It takes a lot of camaraderie for workers to get along at work. However, according to professionals who deal with this issue, incidences of sexual harassment in the workplace are on the rise.

Your daily work life will be more stressful if your workplace is poisonous. We've all had awful weeks or even days at work. A toxic workplace is marked by managers pressuring staff to focus on specific projects, a communication gap between staff and management, and other difficulties.

A few factors that contribute to a burnout work culture include underappreciation, partiality, unhealthy communication, gossiping, and frequent turnover. Ineffective management, a lax code of behaviour, weak leadership, and a lack of communication are also toxic workplace practises.

Such problems are unavoidably present every day in a hostile job. It can lead to problems, disputes, low morale, excessive stress, poor outcomes, sickness, high staff turnover, and even abusive conduct among workers. Conflict arises in an environment that is poisonous, when productivity is also impacted by personal issues.

It is often believed that toxic bosses with inadequate leadership abilities and a lack of credibility are to blame for toxic environments. A toxic employee has an adverse effect on everyone around them, and when they transmit negativity at work, other staff members are more likely to get sick frequently, produce less, and experience stress. The goal of these individuals is to maintain their position of authority, wealth, or special status, or to divert attention from their mistakes and wrongdoings at work.

You've landed your dream job, but are you comfortable with the work environment? There's a chance that you're employed in a harmful environment. While a company's leadership and workplace atmosphere contribute to its success, the same factors may also stifle its expansion. According to surveys, 78% of employees claim that toxic conduct at work has considerably reduced their commitment to the organisation. While the epidemic has forced the workforce to work online, workplace toxicity has also changed as a result. Although remote employment has raised satisfaction by 20%, workplace toxicity is starting to become an issue. Regardless of whether you are underpaid and overworked or dealing with slackers. It's essential to recognise the telltale indications of a toxic environment in the workplace.

- **What is a hazardous work environment?**
- **What factors contribute to a toxic workplace?**
- **Which behaviours indicate a toxic workplace?**
- **What does a work-from-home environment that is poisonous look like?**
- **How can you stay alive in a hostile workplace?**
- **What is a toxic work environment?**

A toxic work environment is one with a bad atmosphere that interferes with the overall efficiency of the organisation and might impact the personal lives of those who are at work. You may experience depression and mental fatigue as a result of a toxic workplace culture, which may eventually have an impact on your physical and mental health. Employees get disengaged at work, and productivity suffers as a result. It causes a rise in staff turnover over time.

What leads to a toxic workplace environment?

You may have questioned what makes a work environment poisonous. The foundation of the problem lies in what makes a workplace poisonous in the first place. Are they senior supervisors, direct reports, or coworkers? Is it a lack of motivation or a high staff turnover rate? A toxic workplace results from the interaction of several elements. Some of the main causes of a toxic workplace are listed below:

The firm has no established set of rules and principles and no core beliefs. Even though the key principles have been stated, nobody on staff demonstrates them. Even if the adjustment does not meet the demands of the workforce, the corporation is unwilling to make it. The organisation lacks effective leadership, and there is little room for input. The workers don't appreciate the values and can't tell the difference between a productive workplace and one that is dysfunctional.

Your mental health might suffer greatly if your employment is poisonous. Depending on the severity of the issue, it has been stated that employees frequently experience anxiety or sadness. But what really qualifies as a hazardous workplace? The following are some indicators of a hazardous or toxic workplace that you should watch out for in any company:

- If you see staff members who are frequently confused, you know your workplace is hazardous. This typically occurs when there is a communication barrier between management and staff members or between coworkers. Speaking and listening are two-way processes that make up communication. You should be aware that one indication of a toxic workplace is if you have a great idea and the corporation won't listen to you.
- In offices, chit-chatting while having a coffee break is customary. You know your employment is poisonous if you overhear others making vulgar jokes or using stereotypical language. Employees frequently create groups and use their inside jokes to make new members feel uncomfortable. Even though it might not be intended, it could make certain individuals feel uneasy and isolated. You don't have to tolerate any of those hazardous workplace indicators, so be on the lookout for them.
- A lack of a visionary leader inside a corporation might result in the development of a poisonous work environment. An unpleasant employer may be to blame if employees frequently quit their jobs at your organisation. If your employer has poor leadership abilities yet wants the business to succeed at the highest level, there may be a toxic work environment.
- The act of appointing friends and coworkers to a position even if they may not be qualified is known as "cronyism." When there are openings at work and

you see that friends, relatives, and alumni are frequently tapped for positions while highly competent candidates who aren't connected to the firm are still awaiting a callback, you know your workplace is toxic.

- Not all instances of a lack of boundaries include colleagues making unpleasant jokes. It may go farther than that, such as when management forces workers to put work before everything else in their lives. These hazardous workplace red flags might show up early if you've just started working there.

- The continual checking in on employees or floor patrols by managers might be interpreted as a lack of trust in the workplace. Employees may eventually start to doubt their own value and their own talents as a result.

- There is a considerable likelihood that a dysfunctional workplace will provide subpar outcomes if your bosses cling on too closely.

- Workplace toxicity occurs when there is a high level of tension at work as a result of an employee error. The workers would thus be frightened to act independently or even to do a good job. Additionally, it would prevent the firm and its personnel from growing normally.

- The only reason people are working in a poisonous environment is to make money. They are not motivated in any way, and you can wind up performing the task that they refuse to do.

- Depending on their disposition, your coworkers may have a favourable or negative influence. If you believe your colleagues are unwilling to help you, If you want to grow and basically laze about, you should think about quitting a poisonous workplace.

- There is no possibility for progress in a toxic environment since all the variables There won't be anything supporting an individual's growth. If your business doesn't seem to be interested in your professional by denying you opportunities for study, movement, or mentoring. chances to develop your career or expertise. Despite the fact that it's Your workplace has a significant impact.

- It's never easy to decide to leave a job, but if your organisation has a history of having staff leave within a short period of time, take that into consideration as one of the indications of a toxic work environment.

- In contrast, one indication of a poisonous workplace culture is if the company adheres to the "hire and fire" policy. A high turnover rate is a sign that the business lacks leadership, fundamental principles, and development opportunities.

- It's never easy to decide to leave a job, but if your organisation has a history of having staff leave within a short period of time, take that into consideration as one of the indications of a toxic work environment.

- You can experience a lack of work-life balance if you frequently feel overwhelmed or must work on your days off. Once you log out of your job, you should be able to enjoy a pleasant, quiet meal.

- Perhaps you should think again about working for that company if you are required to be accessible round-the-clock and are continuously worried about the task. If work takes up the majority of your day, learn to set up appropriate boundaries. Your mental tranquilly is crucial!

- Employees in a toxic workplace experience ongoing pressure to achieve at their highest level and persistent job instability.In contrast, one indication of a poisonous workplace culture is if the company adheres to the "hire and fire" policy. A high turnover rate is a sign that the business lacks leadership, fundamental principles, and development opportunities. One symptom of a toxic workplace is that you worry about work continuously, even while you are having fun with your loved ones. While it's crucial that you understand how to control your stress, the business must take care not to overwork its staff.

- No matter how hard you work for your firm, are your efforts ignored? Most likely, you are shackled to a hazardous workplace. The efforts of employees will not be appreciated or given credit in a chaotic workplace. You will soon experience burnout and a lack of motivation in such a situation. Your working style and mental health will both be affected.

- In a business setting, body language is more effective than words. Take note of how the staff interacts with one another. Do they have a kind, inviting appearance, or does their body language convey a bad attitude?

- You are in the correct position if your coworkers are kind and upbeat toward you, but you should think about changing jobs if they are making nasty remarks, casting contemptuous glances your way, raising their voices, or using threatening body language.

- In any business, employee performance is improved through feedback. One of the warning signs of a toxic workplace is when an organisation is unwilling to accept or provide feedback. If you provide feedback and your coworkers are not as accepting of it, you may also notice resistance to it. In any case, you are aware that the company cannot support your growth.

- You could be wrong if you believe that a poisonous workplace can only be found in a conventional office setting. In a poll done in 2021, over 29% of those who worked remotely believed that despite working remotely, relationships and team spirit had degraded.

Even in a distant context, there is a strong likelihood that rumours will spread since they serve as a working interpersonal link. One indication of a toxic workplace is when coworkers engage in more gossip and fewer productive activities. If you are overflowing with ideas but your voice is not heard in meetings, it could be because you work in a toxic environment. The thoughts of the employees are not valued at work, and only a small group of people make decisions. Negative working conditions include disregarding employees' suggestions, and you should think twice before accepting a position with such a company.

Even though working remotely saves time and effort in areas like commute time, the burden can occasionally be too much. If it just happens sometimes, it may be dealt with, but if you are consistently weighed down by an enormous task, you are trapped in a toxic environment.

Micromanagement tools are widely used in businesses to keep an eye on their employees.These technologies are used by about 78% of businesses to keep an eye on their workers. The method can cause toxicity in the workplace even if its goal is to guarantee that productivity has not yet been compromised. It can give workers the impression that the business doesn't believe in them, which might make them think poorly of it.

You can quickly become irritated if your firm ignores your concerns despite your repeated attempts to communicate them. The communication between management and staff is much more asynchronous when working remotely. Employee concerns are often missed since management isn't confronted by them every day.

How can you live through a toxic workplace?

Knowing the warning signs of a hazardous workplace will enable you to determine whether the company you work for shares these values. If it is, should you quit right away and leave the office to prevent toxic behaviour at work? Take a proactive stance and inform management of your issue as soon as you become aware of it. Reach out to staff to address the issue by providing a solution rather than merely expressing the issue if poor communication is the root of the poisonous environment. Create a setting where receiving feedback is valued, and model this behaviour for your coworkers. If you are concerned about gossip, insist that it not be spread and encourage positive relationships in your office support group. To prevent burnout, be clear about your availability and establish specific timetables related to it. If you've done everything else to lessen workplace toxicity and nothing seems to be working, make a major exit. Instead of quitting right away, it would be preferable to bring the issue up. If you find yourself in a toxic job and are unsure about what to do, the methods listed below can help you survive.

A toxic work atmosphere is created when inclusion, diversity, and ethical behaviour are not promoted. If the organisation lacks fundamental principles or doesn't appear to live by them, that is the main reason for workplace toxicity. Lack of leadership and the inability to receive or offer constructive criticism can exacerbate a poisonous work environment. Excessive gossiping, poor communication, and cronyism are a few telltale indications of a hazardous workplace. If you are unable to set boundaries or trust your coworkers, your job may be toxic. If the employees' concerns are not addressed in meetings and the issues are not resolved, a toxic workplace culture can also exist in a remote work environment.You must express your complaints to management in order to survive a hazardous job. If workers can contribute helpful solutions rather than just pointing out issues, workplace toxicity can be lessened.

Toxic behaviour does not go away just because you are not in direct contact with your coworkers, a particularly toxic employer, or an oppressive work environment. If the atmosphere in your physical workplace was poisonous, it's possible that the same toxic habits will find a way to infiltrate your work-from-home environment. It is better to be as informed as you can be.

How can a poisonous workplace be improved?

When you notice signs of a burnout work culture in your organisation, you must take corrective action. Online office gossip is quite traceable, whether it originates from chat applications, side emails, or post-meeting summaries. Is it terrible news? It continues to be as harmful, useless, and destructive as actual gossip. While it is dumb (that's a good way of saying it) for certain toxic employees to continue to engage in bullying conduct or leave a digital trail of derogatory remarks, they nonetheless do it. You have a few choices if you notice it occurring in your virtual office.

First of all, refrain from any activity that even somewhat resembles gossip. Even though workplace gossip might be fascinating when you're working from home and are bored, it's a pointless waste of time. It might sometimes be challenging to determine whether what you're feeling is genuinely a rumour. According to studies by body language specialist Albert Mehrabian, vocal signals, including tone, account for 38% of a message's effect, while the other 55% is entirely nonverbal. Working online has the benefit of occasionally making it simpler to end poisonous interactions without having to have face-to-face confrontations.

How to prevent your team from working in a toxic environment?

Provide workers who wish to volunteer with a day off each year. Make a drive for back-to-school items for a neighbourhood charity. Or take part in the United Way workplace donation initiative. Employees will notice that you care by taking even the smallest action.

Discuss the idea of increasing the number of feedback meetings with their direct reports and middle and senior managers. They might use this opportunity to praise the person's excellent effort and offer helpful comments. Incorporate frequent employee spotlights and schedule time during your monthly all-hands meeting for employees to thank and honour other team members. Positive reinforcement encourages people, and this approach enables workers to develop deep relationships with their coworkers.

Start hiring with culture in mind. By using this strategy, you can be confident that the prospects you hire will have a genuine connection with your staff. People who offer culture to your team are those who share your basic values and are enthusiastic about your objective while also bringing a distinctive background, viewpoint, or experience. By employing this tactic, you may create a culture that welcomes people from various backgrounds and is diverse.

Start reading those employee evaluations. Start a structured programme to mentor and train people with potential after adding a question that determines whether an employee wants to advance in the organisation.

Make a list of your key values and share it. These should be the predetermined set of values that are actually important to your team and will aid in your goal-achieving. Ensure that C-suite executives, HR officials, and long-term workers are in agreement on core principles before promoting them to the rest of the organisation. The remainder of the team should then discuss each value. By doing this, a coherent business culture will be developed by encouraging positive behaviours and attitudes. To make sure every new hire shares the same principles as your team, go back to your core values during the hiring process.

Develop a plan for employer branding. Although you have little control over how the public perceives your business, you may influence the narrative. Building an appropriate employer brand is obviously crucial, and you can only do so if you first establish a dynamic workplace culture.

Raise the bar and hold everyone accountable. Make sure all team members uphold your core principles, since they are crucial to your culture and the success of your business. Maintaining an open culture based on equality will be facilitated by holding all employees to the same standards. Additionally, by promoting your fundamental principles throughout all departments, you'll help them permeate your culture.

If you see that rumours are spreading more frequently than not, confront the issue. Talk one-on-one to the people who appear to be participating the most. Try to identify them. Additionally, you should formally address the whole staff to let them all know that this conduct will not be condoned.

It's time to intensify your corporate culture approach. But to achieve that, you must comprehend the underlying issue. During exit interviews, ask workers about the reasons they chose to leave. Try to comprehend what about your culture irritated them and what elements they found challenging to give up.

Then, talk to staff members, especially those who have been there for a long time, to find out what has kept them there.Think about doing a poll on employee engagement and thoroughly examining the results. Take action once you've identified what needs to be improved.

You could be placing too much emphasis on performance if you see that people are intensely competitive with one another. Of course you want the best performers on your team, but you also want the whole team to be there. Pitting people against one another will irritate workers and diminish their worth as people.

Recognise performance on a bigger scale and outside the parameters of monetary awards to prevent firing excellent personnel. Encourage managers to give their direct reports recognition for their efforts and to honour their accomplishments with wellness-related rewards like a free exercise class, a gift card to a favourite restaurant, or an additional day off. Create a platform so that people may commend and express their gratitude to their coworkers for a job well done. Employee motivation and a focus on working as a team will increase as a result.

To begin with, make sure middle and senior managers arrive on time each morning. Because workers model their behaviour after their superiors, if one manager frequently arrives 30 minutes late, their direct reports will assume they can do the same. Then, inquire about their work schedule with the repeat offenders. It's probable that they have a consistent conflict that justifies a modified start time, such as dropping their children off at school or commuter limitations.

Improve the way your team manages sick days, medical appointments, and other authorised absences by including the HR department. Of course, you should be willing to talk about private issues and mitigating situations. Together, these strategies will lower your absence rate and foster an environment at work where communication is valued.

Just promote lunch breaks. Start by eating lunch, then encourage staff to take advantage of their break. A wonderful method to enforce a midday break, get to know your staff, and promote employee interaction is to sometimes provide food for the workplace. Additionally, be sure to let new employees know how long they may take a break for lunch. Otherwise, they could decide not to take a break at all.

Acknowledge success in public, make corrections in confidence, and frame the mistake as a chance to improve. Employees who work in a positive atmosphere can make errors without feeling guilty about them.

Talk to management about reevaluating workloads to prevent unnecessarily overworking your staff. Make sure each employee has a sufficient number of tasks to keep them engaged and successfully contribute to the development of the company without causing burnout. You might also need to assess the expectations placed on the entire team; if everyone is working themselves to the bone, it could be possible to add another worker to help with the burden.

Launch company-wide projects and team-building events to get teams interacting and cooperating, even when it's not for business. Information may flow more effectively when it comes to day-to-day work by tearing down these early barriers between teams and even within teams. Furthermore, open-door practises established at the top level may greatly improve communication. When participation and transparency are promoted from the top down, information is less likely to be imprisoned. The effort required to change the communication philosophies ingrained in a company's culture might be challenging, but it will be worthwhile.

Assemble your HR team, establish a diversity, equality, and inclusion policy, and, if necessary, employ a workplace consultant. The phrase "nothing for us, without us" should be kept in mind while creating workplace regulations aimed at ensuring that all employees feel safe doing their jobs. Make the policy known to the staff and encourage them to submit changes by presenting it as a live document.

Don't only focus on what needs to be done; get interested in what your team members need to be innovative and productive. Every manager should be aware of what is required of them to meet the bigger team goals, but they should also pause and consider what is required of their teams to achieve those goals. Every person is different and has different demands. Some people may want better food to feel upbeat and motivated, while others may require more psychological safety or the ability to work from home.

A one-size-fits-all strategy won't be effective. Although you can't have different policies for everyone, it's important to try to accommodate everyone's demands on an individual basis and to be accommodating, especially when it comes to your top priorities. To be interested, one must actively listen, demonstrate empathy, ask questions, and pay attention to what others are saying.

Assign employees to positions that will enable them to do their greatest work to date. You risk asking employees to execute activities that are outside of their scope if you just concentrate on what has to get done. It's wonderful to push people to improve, but it's not healthy to set them up for failure.

The tasks were frequently challenging, exposed participants to some danger, and tested their knowledge and abilities. Similar to this, in order to perform to the best of our skills at work, we must be stretched to the limit. We feel more confident and develop as a result.

However, when you push someone too far, they begin to doubt their abilities and get unmotivated. You will benefit from the boost in productivity that only occurs when people are employing their best skills if you take the time to slow down, figure out what individuals are truly excellent at, and put them in the appropriate roles.

Additionally, they will be more inclined to believe that they are doing their greatest work to yet. By giving their teams the chance to work on various teams or completely different projects, leaders may aid their teams in discovering their strengths. It may be possible to discover hidden abilities by rotating high potentials across various areas and letting them pursue their interests. Keep in mind that everyone desires to believe that they are living out their finest mission. Everybody wants to believe that they are a positive force in the world.

- How can you encourage your workers to understand how important their part is in helping the company improve the world?
- Who does your business serve?
- How can you as workers better people's lives?
- What matters most to your team?
- Who are they trying to please?
- Can you give an example of a "aha" moment that gave you a fresh sense of motivation at work or elsewhere?

According to recent employee survey data, managers are more likely to motivate and retain employees when they link their teams' work to the organisation's larger goals and objectives. Managers may assist their staff put the function they perform in a bigger context and feel less like an anonymous gear in the machine by being interested and having these dialogues.

Corporate cultures are not always harmful. When managers cease having the discussions that make employees feel seen, heard, valued, and involved in, they start acting in that way. The greatest way to deal with toxicity is to have dialogues with your employees about how to meet their needs, allay their worries, find out what drives them, accomplish the finest job of their life, and live out their mission. Only when managers stop focusing so intently on what needs to be done will their staff feel motivated enough to complete everything.

Hold on tight if your organisation uses poor communication practices. Most likely, the environment you're in is poisonous and will only become worse with time. Gossipy behavior, cliques, and exclusion may exist in a toxic workplace. Nobody has stated, "I want the workplace to feel like eighth grade all over again." So it may be rather disheartening when you actually feel like you're back in the cafeteria of your middle school. Everyone knows what a clique looks like. It's the group of folks that stick together, get coffee together, laugh at inside jokes (of which they miraculously have about one million), and generally exclude everyone outside of their close-knit circle—whether at work or in school. And even though we are all adults here, it may be really lonely to be outside of a vibrant clique. Simply put, cliques at work are detrimental to productivity. While making friends and acquaintances at work is a positive thing, it is preferable to steer clear of any actions that may be seen as "clique-ish." Avoid any cliques, bullies at work, or organisations that exclude others. No one wants to return to middle school, despite any potential advantages.

Avoid cliques. Avoid working with gossipy coworkers. Spreading rumours should be avoided. At work, they have no place. If you see that management and executive-level personnel engage in clique-like conduct, you may have an organisational meanness issue, which is about as destructive as it gets.

If you have no other options, poor leadership is an indication of a poisonous environment. The way you act as a leader is crucial. It establishes the standard for how others act at work. You can try discussing these concerns with the HR department or your awful boss's supervisor, if there is one.

Unfortunately, unless you hold a leadership role, this issue is a sign of much more serious issues, and it's doubtful that you will learn or develop in this setting. It's not necessarily your work that gives you inspiration and drive. It could be time for you to move on, though, if you feel entirely stagnant and have nowhere to develop. Rapid turnover is an indication that things are bad or will get worse. Try to talk with some of the workers who departed, were terminated, or were placed on leave if you can.

Maintaining a work-life balance is crucial for survival. No human being should be asked to work nonstop. It's poisonous if your work necessitates constant availability. Your employment is poisonous if your employer expects you to respond to emails in the middle of every Saturday. Yes, occasionally problems do arise at inconvenient times.

However, if your employer expects you to be available at all times, your position is poisonous junk, in our humble view. Setting appropriate work boundaries is a smart approach to staying away from these kinds of toxic work environments. It probably isn't for you if your limits can't be fulfilled, or at least compromised.

Your stomach is your biggest warning indicator, much like when you consume too much sugar or bad food. If anything about your employment makes you feel uneasy, it probably does. There is a serious issue if your anxiety is through the roof, you believe you are the victim of prejudice, your physical health is declining, and all of these things are occurring frequently. Embrace your instincts. If you need a second opinion, ask a friend or family member. But your intuition knows best.

Having your weekly meetings online might make things much worse if you have trouble speaking out at in-person sessions. After all, muting meeting participants serves a purpose. Beyond that, there are the same technological issues that you would have in a face-to-face meeting, such as lag time, interruptions, the "can anybody actually hear me?" problem, and a general lack of eye contact. Successful digital meetings are possible. In fact, teamwork should be much more effective when using video technology properly.

Ask for clarification if you are unable to understand the meaning of a message. Do not interact if what you are seeing is merely a rumour. Gather proof if it's extremely harmful or directed at a specific individual, even you!Talk to your management if you believe that just one person may speak during your remote sessions. Think of ways to schedule meetings so that everyone on the team has a chance to contribute by setting agendas and adhering to them.

Can changing your perspective help you handle stress and negativity?

People don't always have the choice of leaving a less-than-ideal circumstance for a variety of reasons. Finding strategies to manage is essential since you could be forced to stay for far longer than you'd prefer in a toxic workplace. It is more probable to feel claustrophobic in negative work environments since they frequently foster and support a stuck attitude or the idea that nothing ever changes. You are more likely to confront and overcome some of the characteristics of a toxic workplace if you embrace a growth mindset, or the belief that you can still advance by focusing on the things you do have control over.

A growth mindset may thus enable you to emotionally distance yourself from the negative.The key to surviving and succeeding in this atmosphere is realising and understanding that you cannot control what other people say and do, and thinking plays a significant role in this. Keep an eye out for employees who are nagging or spreading rumors. Maintain your composure and place restrictions on how much time and effort you will devote to unproductive activities at work.

It's also critical to constantly remind yourself that you are in charge of your feelings, ideas, and actions. Focusing on and employing healthy coping mechanisms can help you finish your task and prevent interference from outside forces. Think about going for a 15-minute stroll around the block or engaging in some yoga or meditation during your lunch break. To battle the bad sentiments that accumulate during the course of a day in a toxic workplace, try to interact with one positive person each day, put inspirational quotes near your desk, or seek the aid of your partner or friends to take part in enjoyable after-work activities.

You are facing a poisonous workplace culture if micromanagement is encouraged and there is no confidence in your company. Use one of the many employee engagement tools if you don't trust me and see for yourself. Inform the staff at your firm that you will be conducting surveys of them every three months and that they are absolutely confidential. Watch the comments and feedback come in after the initial survey. Continue to encourage your people to express their opinions. Going to work feels unpleasant in toxic workplace cultures. New ideas can't flourish in a poisonous atmosphere; individuals can't be honest; bullying sadly happens; leaders are given authority that may feed their egos; and when leaders ask for questions at town halls or all-hands meetings, it has a strange sensation.

High achievers leave harmful workplace environments. High achievers receive communications from recruiters and rivals peddling the idea that the grass is greener every day on networks like LinkedIn. High achievers have nothing to lose by moving on and trying another organisation if their current one has a poisonous work environment. High performers are aware of their talents and are also perceptive enough to see that, if they can succeed in a firm with a toxic work environment, they can do the same in one that puts its people's needs first. Your organisation may be poisonous if your top performers appear disinterested or lack excitement.

It is impossible to make simple selections that could drive away clients. When it should take minutes, a simple refund for a customer who never received the service they paid for takes weeks. A choice cannot be made when a product has to be changed because consumers are leaving in droves. Making no decision at all is simpler than admitting that something has to change. Working from home or part-time is viewed as being unmotivated. Because they want to keep an eye on individuals, management prohibits workers from working remotely. When you work from home, you'll be less efficient and more likely to abuse the position. The possibility that you may have a newborn child at home and choose not to make the daily two-hour journey so you can work more is disregarded. Then, employees who desire to work part-time but are unable to do so because of a side business, children, or a second job are labelled as "lazy."

The truth is that working part-time or from home is not indicative of laziness. Both types of employment allow individuals to have lives, and if you let them, they will show you loyalty and dedication to their jobs.

Because it is such a typical method of working, excluding part-time employment or working from home drastically reduces your talent pool. You don't become a high performer or a valuable asset by being tethered to a desk in an office; you become one by being given the freedom to be flexible and treated like a human.

Because they are so terrified that they will leave their jobs and steal their ideas, toxic workplace cultures despise business owners and intrapreneurs. Successful workplace cultures treat employees with prior company ownership experience as their hidden weapons. They encourage entrepreneurship because they want individuals to feel empowered to make decisions and feel like it is their business. Take advantage of entrepreneurs while you still have them, and if they depart, wish them well. Keep in mind that entrepreneurs are the reason why firms are founded in the first place. You have a serious issue if there are consequences for poor performance. Shaming workers won't improve their performance; instead, it will make them despise the company's leadership team even more. When your culture stinks, you'll have more meetings asking, "Why are we not earning money?" and this animosity will subsequently be focused towards your consumers.

People are referred to as traitors when they decide to leave or admit they are considering leaving. In hazardous workplaces, it is typical and appropriate for employees to depart frequently. There are no exit interviews or inquiries into the reasons why a certain leader has lost so many followers so quickly. The justification is always the same: "The boss was terrible, so it's a good thing he is going." Staff members don't stay with the firm for very long, according to a LinkedIn search of the organisation's employees. Requesting employees to post favourable evaluations online to hide the toxicity Yes, that does occur. Former employees who leave scathing evaluations on websites like GlassDoor are an easy way to spot toxic workplaces.

When there is a toxic workplace environment, business owners worry and attempt to hide their mistakes by urging personnel to post fluffy, phoney, and untrue evaluations online to mask the negative ones. A poisonous work environment cannot be concealed; it can only be changed by acknowledging it and altering how you interact with others. Values are rarely discussed. They are described on the corporate website and brought up during the yearly conference, but they are never discussed in relation to regular work. The values are overlooked while speaking with a customer or making a choice. You can't even get hired in a successful culture unless you can show that you uphold the ideals.

Employees have a right to an environment free from toxic and troublesome behaviour; this is not a perk. Since many of us spend more waking hours at work than at home, every employee in any organisation should feel secure and content in their surroundings.

CHAPTER TWO

Diagnosing the Organisational Culture in Workplace Bullying and Harassment

"If a person encounters negative individuals in his life, then he has to work on his own nature rather than that of others, because the amount of toxicity around him is determined by his own fundamental basis."

A toxic work environment is the most common reason for resignation. An expert in risk management describes the characteristics of a toxic workplace environment and how managers might respond with a strategy for change. Toxic is a harsh word that no firm wants to be used to describe the atmosphere at work. Unfortunately, it appears that workplace toxicity is increasing. Perhaps this is because employees are finally feeling confident enough to call it what it has always been. According to recent MIT

Sloan research, toxic work environments are the leading cause of resignation. You may have some questions to be answered.

- **What is the workplace culture?**
- **What constitutes a healthy workplace culture?**
- **What will be the advantages of a supportive work environment?**
- **What does "toxic work culture" mean?**
- **How to build actual instances of workplace culture?**
- **Does the national work culture differ?**
- **How do you foster a supportive work environment?**

Only 60 businesses from the Fortune 500 list in 1955 were still present in 2017. The cause? Many. One of the most significant is dissatisfied employees.

Yes, failing to maintain employee motivation and satisfaction is one of the main reasons that nine out of ten of these businesses fail or combine. They had a poisonous workplace environment that quickly became intolerable for practically every employee. To be honest, before 2010, a poisonous work environment was as prevalent as a cab today. Only a select few companies, like Google, Netflix, and a few others, were prepared to invest in and work toward enhancing employee happiness. Look at them right now! We want the same for you; therefore, I'll discuss the indicators of a toxic workplace culture and their remedies based on our collective experience. There is no filler in this. Only workable solutions that we and our clients have really employed So let's get started. You know, reading might go well with a strong cup of coffee.

A toxic workplace culture may have an impact on the performance of the organisation in addition to the employees since it weakens the workforce and reduces productivity. Similar to a virus, toxicity spreads. Teamwork fails, people lose faith in one another, and growing insecurity can reduce productivity. The antithesis of development, creativity, and innovation is toxic culture. If there is constant conflict, office drama, and disgruntled workers, it creates a toxic work environment that compromises everyone's wellbeing and productivity. Few key warning indicators to watch out for at work are included in the list below.

As a leader, you must prioritise the creation of a positive workplace culture. It is one of the tenets that prosperous businesses like Facebook adhere to. Culture will alter and evolve; therefore, it's important to monitor it and make adjustments as needed. The components of a toxic work environment may occasionally be obvious and simple to change, but they may also be concealed, in which case leaders must consistently endeavour to find them.

Organisational culture: What is it?

Few things are as crucial—and occasionally as hard to understand—as an organisation's culture. In order to assess whether they would "fit in," prospective workers want to know what the culture is like. Customers want to know what to anticipate from interactions with staff. We all desire to understand our origins, identities, and futures. Senior management is interested in learning about the corporate culture so they may utilise it to influence behaviour.

Being a nontoxic workplace is not sufficient; that is only neutral. Instead, businesses should try to create an environment where leaders genuinely listen to their stakeholders, workers, and consumers. Such a culture demands work and persistence to develop. Management must maintain its progress and seek to create a better working environment. Leaders can't merely promise to accomplish anything. They must lead the change and take initiative to put their words into practise.

A strong employee voice is essential. Leadership won't be able to bring about significant change without recognising what is or isn't working. It seems logical that employees are looking for new options and healthier work conditions as the Great Resignation continues. Employers must be open and honest about areas in which their workplace culture needs to be detoxed and then take urgent action to make work work for everyone.

Unsurprisingly, there are several distinct conceptions of corporate culture. Certain characteristics, such as being "innovative," "performance-based," or "traditional," are used to characterise business culture. Others use a dynamic viewpoint, viewing the notion of culture as the interaction of many forces inside the institution. Both methods see culture as a kind of guiding force that directs and moulds an organisation. Although there are several definitions of corporate culture, according to Gallup, culture is essentially "how we do things around here.

Therefore, it should not be surprising that each business has an own culture.We at Gallup approach culture from a practical standpoint. Our experience has shown us that corporate culture and the elements that make it up are intrinsically neutral. The culture of each organisation is distinct and emergent. Every organisation has a unique past and future objectives, and each should be reflected in the business's culture. The first and arguably simplest stage in the cultural journey is defining the culture you desire. But the most important aspects of a company's culture are its "why" and "how."

Every manager should be aware of what is required of them to meet the bigger team goals, but they should also pause and consider what is required of their teams to achieve those goals. Every person is different and has different demands. Some people may want better food to feel upbeat and motivated, while others may require more psychological safety or the ability to work from home. A one-size-fits-all strategy won't be effective. Although you can't have different policies for everyone, it's important to try to accommodate everyone's demands on an individual basis and to be accommodating, especially when it comes to your top priorities. To be interested, one must actively listen, demonstrate empathy, ask questions, and pay attention to what others are saying.

Humans' innate biological and behavioural reactions to fear are widely known. Fight, flight, and freeze in the workplace manifest as resource hoarding, project-defeating competition, and excessive deadlines established by supervisors.

According to our study, these actions are virtually always the outcome of an unspoken fear of shortage and a scarcity mindset. When employees are under stress or uncertain about their position, they tend to fall into these behaviours. When we talk freely and honestly about our worries, they are frequently reduced. To help people feel psychologically comfortable talking about their anxieties in a work environment, the leader must first disclose their own worries. Many of the poisonous behaviours that have been appearing will disappear on their own once the entire team is able to discuss fear openly.

- **What worries are keeping you from moving forward?**
- **What is your default action when you're under stress?**

Most individuals desire success, knowledge, or a sense of giving back. However, if carried too far, any of these fundamental drivers might backfire. Too much emphasis on winning might encourage dishonest behavior. Frustration might result from spending an excessive amount of time reading and studying and not really accomplishing anything. In the correct situation, wanting to assist others is fantastic, but when one stops meeting their own needs in order to do so, it may turn into destructive people-pleasing. People will be more motivated if you understand what they truly desire for them, but you must watch out that they don't receive too much of a good thing.

Someone who craves independence may aggressively oppose or sabotage coworkers who want to work with them if you give them too much room. People readily veer into poisonous territory when their needs get in the way (when they are highly competitive or always seeking approval, for example). Managers must focus on spotting the first indications of toxic conduct. House fires are difficult to put out, whereas minor flare-ups are.

What does "workplace culture" actually mean?

The term "workplace culture" describes the standards of behaviour that apply to a group of people that work together in a particular workplace, such as a team, department, or entire company. Everyone involved in its construction, from the CEO to the newest employees, does so through their deeds. The physical environment of a business has an effect on the workplace culture as well. The relationships, attitudes, beliefs, traditions, and values that occur inside each organisation shape its culture. We would expect that since we spend so much time in the workplace environment, it would have a big effect on us. The idea of workplace culture is not static; rather, it evolves through time in reaction to employee behaviour. The four fundamental types of organisational culture, which is a subset of workplace culture, are clan, adhocracy, hierarchy, and market.

Employees have more options than ever before in a highly competitive job market, so they don't have to settle if their present workplace is unpleasant, risky, or immoral. Job switching no longer only affects Millennials (if it ever did). In comparison to Millennials (5%), Gen X (3%), and Baby Boomers (6%), Gen Z employees spend a full 65% of their time in a position for less than a year. They are also more than twice as likely to quit their present position within the next month (13%).

The company's culture, which is defined as the general ethos of the workplace as well as the principles and policies that guide managers' leadership of employees, may either be its greatest asset or its most dangerous vulnerability. The secret is to watch out for the telltale indicators of a poisonous workplace environment and act to change it.

You must relearn the habits that hold you back daily. To learn to fly, you must get rid of your negativity.

It may not be feasible to have a toxic-free workplace, but you can learn how to deal with it properly. Learn how to survive in or leave a hostile workplace. Conflict, anxiety, and fury are abundant in toxic groups. People respond physiologically to their surroundings as though they are in a fight-or-flight scenario. People who are healthy go ill. More people have colds, the flu, and stress-related ailments, including heart attacks. In contrast, sick days are used less frequently, and turnover is lower in resilient businesses. People joke about, grin, and are friendly to one another.

- **How to determine whether an environment is healthy or toxic?**
- **How to determine quickly whether a serious issue exists without spending all of your time listening to complaints?**
- **Why investigations alone are insufficient to address complaints at work?**
- **How to effectively respond to complaints?**

The effects of a toxic workplace are extensive. It causes worry, strife, and tension. Physical and emotional well-being are both jeopardized.It ruins connections. Your soul, though, is what the poisonous workplace attacks most.

Working in a toxic environment may cause stress, fatigue, depression, harm to your self-esteem, and significant disturbances to your daily routine. So, if you're wondering if your job issues are the product of generalised work stress or something worse and you found this post, let's delve into symptoms that your workplace may be very dysfunctional. To increase accessibility, we also produced a movie that lists the indicators of a toxic workplace. If any of these apply to your job, it's time to make changes, or you might consider looking for a more wholesome place to work.

It spreads quickly when someone has a good attitude and a high level of motivation. People are more productive and joyful at work when they all smile, speak kindly to one another, and exchange jokes—not insults disguised as humour. Sadly, the inverse is also accurate. A toxic workplace may be to blame if you notice that everyone in the office has poor morale. I'm talking about a situation where there always seems to be a dark cloud over the workplace, with persistent low energy and joylessness at work. Forget the Monday blues and the rare terrible days.

The fact that communication typically only happens in one direction—as orders from management to staff—is a telltale symptom of a poisonous workplace environment. Employees are hesitant to seek clarification because they fear being singled out for not grasping concepts quickly enough or because nothing will be done. This, among many other factors, may result in time loss and duplication of labor. The boss is feared by the workforce. There is a distinction between a healthy respect for the boss and outright terror. There is an issue with the culture when no one but the boss talks during meetings and when individuals avoid walking down the hallway where they could run into the boss.

Policies are put in place to help people, but a company

that consistently prioritises policies above people risks developing a toxic work environment. People make errors, whether you like it or not, and even the greatest staff won't be able to accomplish everything correctly all the time, so you need to provide room for that. If management punishes every infringement or departure from rules, your workplace has a poisonous culture since this frequently results in stressed-out workers who are reluctant to take chances.

This is possibly one of the most obvious signs of a toxic workplace. People continue to depart. There's probably a problem with your company culture when it turns into a walk-through office. Yes, it is acceptable for employees to seek better opportunities, but if you have to recruit people all year, some after they've only been with you for a few months, something is clearly wrong with the workplace culture.

Have you ever brought a concern to your supervisor or human resources manager that they could only sympathise with but that they recognised as a problem?

People naturally gravitate toward others with whom they share interests. This should not come as a surprise because many individuals have the best buddies at work. But in a poisonous workplace environment, these cliques and groupings are rife with conflict and rivalry. When these cliques engage in sabotage, backstabbing, and blackmail, competition ceases to be healthy. Bosses isolating themselves, dining alone, and completely cutting off the staff makes sense in a terrible workplace where everyone is forced to establish their own cliques. When creating your corporate culture, avoid doing stuff like this.

For two reasons, this is a classic indicator of a toxic workplace environment. The first is that a single, small number of inaccessible employers have all the sway. Employees are unable to advance since there is no delegation, which also prevents them from becoming empowered. The second is that the employees must look out for themselves because no one is watching out for them. There is no method for employees to receive assistance if they need it.

Employee indifference or the creation of their own regulations to get around their superiors' oppressive and impractical restrictions might result from this. An employee who is aware that they will not be permitted to request a day off for a valid reason will instead fabricate a sick day excuse. In conclusion, employees are frequently the victims of a toxic work environment. While management is responsible for defining the culture and making any required corrections, they are more likely to succeed if they solicit input from and include the workforce. After all, culture is created by people.

Toxic individuals bind themselves to your ankles like cinder blocks and then urge you to swim in their contaminated waters.

Culture is more than simply the benefits and initiatives created by HR. Culture change can only be achieved if all parties take responsibility for the problem and are dedicated to solving it. This entails correcting the unfavourable working practises or standards that have facilitated employee disease or low well-being. Most importantly, safer substitutes should be used in their place.

What are the primary elements of a company's culture?

What are the main factors influencing culture, and how can leadership employ these factors to quicken cultural change?

The five most important factors influencing corporate culture have been identified by Gallup based on our decades of experience with organisational transformation and culture-building. Together, these factors influence how employees behave, make choices, and complete their tasks. Can the culture of an organisation change? By employing a comprehensive approach to assessing and controlling culture, organisations may develop and maintain a strong corporate culture that fosters high performance.

Four Steps for Culture Change
1. Recognise your culture's current state.
2. Identify the cultural difference between your ideal and the real world.
3. Align systems, initiatives, and activities.
4. Establish continual evaluation and accountability.

Without a strategy for a positive workplace culture, it's all too simple to fall back on at least some elements of a poisonous environment.

Examine the culture of the workplace today. In the initial stage of our study, we consulted with top-level executives from throughout the firm to help them reach consensus on the ideal corporate culture. Leaders must agree on the true nature of the ideal corporate culture if a business is to successfully transform the culture at work.

As in so many other aspects of life, prevention is always preferable to treatment. There are ways for a business or leader to change the situation and concentrate on creating a positive and professional environment that will keep their current employees and draw in new ones. I think it's critical to find any negative actors early on and tackle the issue before it worsens. Following that, you should put your strategy into action to address any problems in order to prevent the same errors or issues from occurring again. Being deliberate about boosting employee involvement is one of the best strategies to prevent toxic cultures.

An anonymous employee feedback system is a terrific way to get feedback from your staff on the policies you've set in place, and it also gives staff members a mechanism to report any wrongdoing they overhear or observe at work. This enables leadership to get open input from staff members and take appropriate measures to transform the culture. Don't make the adjustments you do make after that a surprise. You should inform your staff of any changes to business rules and practises so that everyone is aware of the new expectations.

In almost every business, there is a discrepancy between what management claims the corporate culture and values are and what people perceive them to be. In the second stage, we assess where the desired culture of leaders and the culture that employees experience are aligned and where they are not. We present a report to the leadership that highlights areas of consistency, alignment, and clarity as well as possible commitment-blocking factors. Our strength of identity report contrasts the aspirational culture of leaders with the actual culture that their workforce encounters. When accessible, it also contains other indicators, including information on organisational performance and employee engagement. This study offers a quantitative explanation of the sometimes elusive connection between culture and productivity.

To create an action plan for modifying and reshaping cultural expectations, we collaborate with leaders. This calls for different things from different firms. For some, it entails realigning performance measures to the intended purpose and brand; for others, it begins with bettering core message delivery.

Whatever the starting position of a company, our aim is to determine how rapidly it wants to advance and together develop a road map to get there. Cultural transformation, in my opinion, takes time. While companies that work to increase employee engagement frequently see improvements within a year, those that focus on changing company culture typically experience the greatest improvements after three to five years. Gallup and the organisation's leadership build efficient monitoring and accountability indicators to ensure constant success. To track and evaluate progress toward the intended state, Gallup provides a variety of standard measures as well as customised indicators. The most significant action that firms can take in the long run is to consistently monitor the appropriate elements of company culture. By area, business unit, and job, scientifically based measurement evaluates how the company's mission, brand, and culture are evolving.

Effective assessment and monitoring tools uncover business units that lack a strong relationship to the aspirational state as well as units that are more vulnerable to risk, whether it be via turnover, low productivity, compliance issues, or poor customer service. Under the advice of Gallup, leadership should examine culture measurements with other metrics, such as employee engagement and your organisation's specific key performance indicators.

Your company's best culture will be distinctive. Based on preconceived notions of "excellent business culture" or "poor company culture," many culture survey tools make an effort to categorise firms into certain "categories" of corporate culture. These surveys miss the unique characteristics of an organisation because they confine it to a predetermined box. Instead, they push it to conform to others, which results in the loss of its individuality. If each organisation's culture is distinct, it must be self-described, not merely categorised.

Furthermore, most surveys do not approach culture functionally, that is, as the manifestation of an organisation's distinctive mission and identity. Leaders are unsure of what to do after sharing the findings of a general culture index survey with their staff. Finally, rather than taking into account the leadership's own hopes and objectives, a typical organisational culture study compares business culture to outside standards. While a benchmark like this might show how a company stacks up against a benchmark, it would miss the mark on what makes an organisation's culture really distinctive and important. For instance, a lot of businesses include "client centricity" as one of their objectives. But depending on the sector of the market, the type of product or service being offered, and other factors, there are a wide range of ways they might achieve customer centricity.

As a result, measuring only standard items produces only minor improvements in customer-centricity. It offers no indication of how far we have come toward a unique and worthwhile consumer proposal. Your organisational culture survey questions must be adaptable enough to recognise organisational uniqueness, meaningfully connected to internal business operations, and based on well-researched science. Do problems with your workplace culture threaten the health of your employees? Most likely, you've heard of jobs with opulent offices, perks, and even expensive social gatherings. However, despite the well-kept appearance, the workplace atmosphere is poisonous; workers are constantly disengaged and burned out.

Exactly why is corporate culture so crucial?

It's clear that when CEOs miscalculate the value of a company's culture, business performance suffers. Your company's culture is the distinctive manner in which it fulfils its corporate mission and keeps its brand promise to customers. A strong company culture serves as a differentiator in the marketplace because of this. It is the unique manner in which you draw in consumers, keep them around, and persuade them to recommend your brand to others. Additionally, it's a strategy for luring in top personnel and converting them into brand advocates. According to our customers' experiences, teams and people that are most in line with the business culture routinely outperform those who are least in line in terms of internal performance indicators.

- World-class talent is drawn to your business because of its culture.
- Alignment is created through culture.
- Culture places a premium on engaging employees.
- Culture has an impact on output.
- Despite the obvious advantages of a strong business culture, it is important to remember that not all cultural factors directly influence performance measures.

For instance, a "fun" culture may be highly valued by an organisation's leadership. But can a positive work environment genuinely boost productivity? It varies. Each corporation trying to develop its own ideal corporate culture must thus link culture measures to internal key performance indicators. Strengths include inclusivity, diversity, safety, innovation, compliance, and high performance. Leaders must accurately define, measure, and routinely monitor both the culture of their firm and its link to the most crucial performance measures in order to reap the advantages of a strong corporate culture.

Employee behaviour and performance change when they are confident that their leaders are fair, egalitarian, and inclusive.

Employee behaviour and performance change when they are confident that their leaders are fair, egalitarian, and inclusive. When it comes to the success of DEI, perceptions count. Which views of fairness and inclusion, then, ultimately influence employee motivation and business performance? We look at the key elements of efficient DEI measurements in our most recent DEI study, Advancing DEI Initiatives: A Guide for organisational leaders. We also identify four important questions that leaders should respond to in order to develop successful, long-term DEI efforts.

Good corporate culture doesn't just happen. Leaders who learn how to enhance business culture and constantly endeavour to drive change are frequently those who create and nurture it.

Take a look at a few culture-related issues that frequently affect leadership teams: Recent mergers and acquisitions have failed to deliver on their promises. Employees are not significantly affected by a costly endeavour to establish a new goal, purpose, or set of values. When a poor customer experience generates widespread media coverage, CEOs become more intent on enhancing company culture.

Problems with culture can occasionally be overlooked at first. They may only be seen as a pervasive but rising worry that "we are not who we once were." Inability to recruit top people; trouble generating organic growth based on interactions between customers and employees; leadership; an erosion of brand identity in the marketplace and inside the business; diminishing consumer engagement feedback. Leadership initiatives that are failing. At its worst, a dysfunctional culture chips away at your consumer base as people stop believing in or recommending your company to their friends. Employees that are unable to understand the significance of their everyday jobs are eating away at your talent.

What exactly does "toxic work culture" refer to?

Conflicts, drama, office politics, and disgruntled workers are signs of a toxic workplace culture, which has an adverse effect on both employee productivity and welfare.A ccording to media sources, Twitter workers were told on November 3 that they would get an email concerning their employment status the next morning.

According to Twitter, if an employee's work was affected, an email would be sent to their corporate or official mail IDs; if they were fired, an email would be sent to their private IDs. Next, the California-based Twitter cut approximately half of its workforce, or about 3,700 employees. Additionally, Twitter India let off 90% of its Indian employees as part of Elon Musk's global layoffs. About 70% of the engineering and product development positions in India, which were involved in international projects, were eliminated. Numerous fired workers were called again, according to a Bloomberg story, since some were let go by mistake and others were let go before management realised their expertise and knowledge may help Musk develop new features for the website.

There are several indicators of a toxic workplace culture, including internal conflict, dysfunctional behaviour, poor communication, power struggles, and low morale. Furthermore, it does not prioritise employee welfare in its policies and practises. This may take many different forms inside an organisation, and each toxic workplace has its own unique set of issues. There are certain widespread issues, nonetheless, that toxic workplaces may encounter. A low mood, this is not just the Monday morning blues; there is a consistent lack of excitement throughout the entire company. Studies show that negativity spreads quickly and that top performers leave their jobs at a rate that is 13 times higher than that of regular employees.

Your organisation's culture is not a one-time thing. Even after you address a poor corporate culture, you should constantly assess your culture to identify areas for development.

By evaluating employee engagement and routinely soliciting input from your team, you can determine how strong your corporate culture is. Additionally, there are several strategies for businesses to actively promote a pleasant workplace culture. For instance, schedule time for events like team lunches or icebreakers that allow individuals to take a break from their daily responsibilities and mingle with others on their particular team or in other departments. Do not neglect your business culture obligations; keep in mind that your diligence will be rewarded in the long run.

The tasks were frequently challenging, exposed participants to some danger, and tested their knowledge and abilities. Similar to this, in order to perform to the best of our abilities at work, we must be stretched to the limit. We feel more confident and develop as a result. However, when you push someone too far, they begin to doubt their abilities and get unmotivated. You will benefit from the boost in productivity that only occurs when people are employing their best skills if you take the time to slow down, figure out what individuals are truly excellent at, and put them in the appropriate roles.

Additionally, they will be more inclined to believe that they are doing their greatest work yet. By giving their teams the chance to work on various teams or completely different projects, leaders may aid their teams in discovering their strengths. It may be possible to discover hidden abilities by rotating high-potential students across various areas and letting them pursue their interests. Keep in mind that everyone desires to believe that they are living out their finest mission. Everybody wants to believe that they are a positive force in the world.

- **How can you encourage your workers to understand how important their part is in helping the company improve the world?**
- **Who does your business serve?**
- **How can you as workers better people's lives?**
- **What matters most to your team?**
- **Who are they trying to please?**

According to recent employee survey data, managers are more likely to motivate and retain employees when they link their teams' work to the organisation's larger goals and objectives. Managers may assist their staff put the function they perform in a bigger context and feel less like an anonymous gear in the machine by being interested and having these dialogues.

We put a lot of time into our jobs. But occasionally we fail to consider how working and the workplace in general make us feel amid the flurry of deadlines and desk lunches. **Do you ever feel emotionally and physically spent after working all day, or do you ever wake up wishing your workday was over?**

You must have encountered a work environment that was less than ideal if you've ever had at least a few different jobs, since this may have had a negative impact on your general health, happiness, and productivity. And even though most organisations have moments of negativity or toxic behaviour, being able to react and respond effectively during those trying times may help you get the most out of a situation.

It is easy to see when a work environment has deteriorated when morale is low and production has dropped. However, there are several warning indicators to watch out for before things deteriorate to that point, so you can leave the area before it's too late. The absence of a work-life balance, a lack of support, unprofessional coworkers, a lack of leadership, or losing interest in going to work are some indications that your workplace is toxic or is starting to become toxic. Additionally, you can observe a lack of communication, inconsistent standards and practises, and a leader who believes they are above the law.

People who work in toxic environments frequently struggle to distinguish between a bad day and a poisonous workplace. Here's a tip: If your workday is full of employees belittling each other, passive-hostile communication, groups of individuals talking, or cattiness, there's a high likelihood your situation has become more than just annoyance or frustration.

"Customers will never love a company until the employees love it first."

In research published in June 2021, the British Medical Journal identified these effects of toxic work environments. This outcome is concerning at a time when mental health problems are increasing at an unprecedented rate. As we'll see, there was a toxic workplace environment there even before the epidemic.

However, there was no focus on doing additional research or exercising greater skepticism. Now, things have been permanently altered. Problems with one's mental health are more than just an excuse to take a day off. It exists and may be made worse by a hostile workplace environment. At SurveySparrow, we take great pleasure in being a company that puts its employees first. And it falls on us to handle the many indications and remedies of a toxic workplace environment. Without further ado, here are the warning indicators of a poisonous workplace culture that need to be identified and addressed right now. It's time to release the trapped cat.

A strategy that is patchwork-like, lacks cultural congruence, and does more harm than good when leadership teams fail to perceive their culture holistically and fail to pinpoint the key determinants of their ideal business culture.

What is commonly referred to as a "toxic work culture" is frequently an unclear culture. When multiple parts of your business send out contradictory signals, your culture gets muddled. Marketing messages do not align with performance-based incentives for employees. Employee onboarding instructions differ from those provided in management training. Employee conduct is not consistent with leadership's actions. Misalignment is another factor in the failure of work culture change in most firms. New initiatives frequently alter just one part of the culture while maintaining the existing framework. Or they choose to be only cosmetic and do not alter the rigid guidelines that govern their poisonous workplace culture, such as the hierarchical structure, the performance rewards, or the management standards.

When a corporation fails to place any emphasis on having some fundamental corporate values, a poisonous work environment develops. These businesses just care about growing their earnings. And if doing so necessitates overlooking employee satisfaction, fine. These organisations serve as the cradles of a poisonous workplace culture when workers lack a sense of agency and have their needs disregarded. Without clearly stated basic principles, the workplace culture will develop aimlessly. Unwanted subcultures will develop as a result, which will eventually harm the company.

So, you see, it's okay to start off without a business culture. As a leader, you prioritised economic expansion and postponed the cultural issue. But the year to do it is 2021. Create a list of the essential corporate principles you believe the firm should uphold by sitting down with your team leaders and conducting a brainstorming session. Make sure the team leaders have discussed this in advance with each team member. This brainstorming process is crucial because it will bring your company's ideals and the values of its employees closer together. The intersection of these two would provide the guiding principles of your company. Then, use these during the hiring process to confirm that each new employee shares the same values.

If your manager doesn't give you full creative freedom at work, work will quickly become monotonous, and the workplace will become completely poisonous. This warning flag is particularly alarming since employees will imitate their bosses' behaviour if they don't uphold the company's core principles. They'll begin to disregard all morals and develop a mistrust of their leaders since they won't be held accountable for their actions. Their authority will gradually lose credibility, and a distinct gap between the leadership group and the remainder will appear. A poisonous workplace culture at its worst!

This is a problem that SurveySparrow also encountered. In some instances, our team leaders weren't treating our workforce's diversity with the respect we wanted them to. They and the rest of their squad developed a lot of resentment as a result. Senior management initially met with these managers to go through our expectations in detail. They were given time to correct their mistakes after being instructed on proper team leader etiquette. After that, we held leadership training workshops for each of our teams to encourage diversity and equality at work. An employee pulse survey was conducted to determine what lessons were learned from the event by everyone who attended, including CXOs and new hires. The issue was quickly resolved!

In recent years, anonymous review sites like Glassdoor have greatly increased employees' authority. They can be open and honest about their interactions with their current or former employers. As a leader, you must be cautious since this might damage the reputation of the company. Positive feedback, however, can also result in better growth prospects. Therefore, it's a two-edged sword that we've only recently become aware of. Your corporate culture is admired for many different reasons, so it wasn't a problem for you, but you weren't taking advantage of getting good ratings.

So, work on attracting people who are better and better, along with your HR staff. Although you have little control over how the general public views your business, you do have some influence over the daily experiences that staff members have there. Make sure that merits praise and a favourable evaluation. Innovative incentives, powerful and futuristic training sessions, and placing a priority on staff well-being over business objectives will work for you.

Errors are made by employees. That is a fact that cannot be avoided. Sometimes the error is rather bad. However, a company's culture of open criticism is a blatant indication of a poisonous workplace. This is due to the psychological and emotional effects that public humiliation has on a victim. They place unneeded stress on themselves to do things well, losing their originality in the process. Employees in these companies are just concerned with finishing the task at hand; they are not concerned with producing outcomes. In essence, they quit taking chances to avoid getting criticised in public.

The fix is rather straightforward. Quit voicing criticism in public. Yes, refrain from openly criticising an employee. Reserve it for private discussions. Be sure to publicly laud them for their excellent efforts. Call them to your office to discuss anything improper they may have done. Employees will be able to improve by learning from their failures in such a positive work atmosphere.

If you only acknowledge the top sales performer(s) of each quarter while dismissing the efforts of the others, you are harming the culture and creating a toxic workplace environment. It is a certain method to create toxic work environments to recognise and reward a select few people from a limited number of domains. I'm saying this because the remainder of your staff, which doesn't feel appreciated for its job, is disengaged. They lose the drive to continue working hard, which eventually slows both their own and the organisation's growth. I would call that a very clear warning flag.

Do you know why individuals are ecstatic to join the dominant search engine, Google? And why do their employees never say anything unfavourable about them? In fact, as part of their employee death benefits program, they pay the widow of a deceased employee 50% of their income for ten years in a row. That's your prize, huh? Your greatest strength as a leader is empathy. And in terms of employee recognition and rewards, it ought to dominate. In 2021 and beyond, monetary incentives, gift cards, and year-end raises won't cut it. It's time to get creative with appreciation programmes if you think that keeping staff content is the key to achieving long-term company objectives. Start by analysing employee input before personalising the entire process of gratitude and reward. Then, every employee would think they were providing the greatest service possible. The perfect scenario would be this, wouldn't it?

High employee turnover has cost businesses $223 billion over the last five years. $223 billion, that amount certainly warrants concern. Employees quitting their jobs due to a poisonous workplace environment are reason for concern, as opposed to those quitting their jobs to take on a new challenge or launch their own business. Employees that are still there don't take the company seriously because of its terrible culture. If they feel that the culture is not appropriate, more than one-third of American workers are willing to reject the "ideal job." Employees being let go left and right would be an obvious sign of a hostile workplace environment.

You must return to the discussion and continue to work on the corporate culture plan. Finding the cause of the issue must come first. The best method for doing it is through exit interview surveys. You will then comprehend the issue with your corporate culture and how it is resulting in a poisonous work environment. The next step should be talking to the staff, especially the long-term employees, to determine what has kept them there. The solution here would be to conduct and analyse an employee engagement survey. Last but not least, take the necessary action.

Healthy competition is excellent for both firms and employees. Employees are encouraged to perform at a high level deserving of praise, which benefits both them and the company. A warning indication for a poisonous workplace culture is, however, the presence of competitiveness in the workplace culture. Why? This is due to the fact that such rivalry undermines collaboration and encourages employees to adopt an autonomous mindset. They stop caring about or contributing to the general development of the business, their team, or a colleague in favour of concentrating only on their personal interests. They become hostile toward one another as a result, which is an obvious symptom that something is wrong.

If you value performance too highly, it will result in employees who are overly competitive. It's okay, at least in part. After that, it most definitely isn't. Therefore, this is where the process of correction ought to begin. If the methods of appreciation and rewards exclusively entail monetary benefits, they should be examined and revised. Innovative incentives and compliments, such as publicly praising an employee for assisting a colleague with a task or awarding gift certificates for winning an intramural baseball game, would go a long way toward fostering a sense of camaraderie and collaboration among the team members. They'll continue to be aggressive, but in the proper way.

Employees who are frequently absent from work are clearly showing signs of a problem with the business culture, which is steadily poisoning the environment. An organisation suffers from absenteeism in two separate ways. Employees get disengaged when the workplace culture is unhealthy or poisonous, and their teammates suffer when employees are careless or unconcerned with their jobs. 40% of employees said that the corporate culture played a role in their choice of employer. This statistic, which stood at 37% in 2020, shows that unusual employee absence indicates a poisonous work environment is developing in your organisation.

Start by ensuring that high and middle management are setting the correct examples for timeliness. This is because team leaders influence their subordinates' learning, so you wouldn't want a leader who wasn't committed to the job. Following that, ensure that your HR department meets with employees who frequently take absences and asks them why. If it's true, it will be resolved eventually; if not, the HR staff will be aware of the issue that the employee is facing. In order to guarantee that leaves for legitimate reasons are issued without difficulty, the HR department can strive to strengthen the sick day tracking sheet for your team. This simple change would significantly increase employee happiness. We say this based on personal experience. You'll see if you try it.

Office rumours are frequently not taken as seriously as they ought to be. Many organisations view it as acceptable. Undoubtedly, some of it is okay, but too much of it can be problematic. We're referring to rumours that spread around the workplace and cause conflict between coworkers. The workplace develops a culture of factions over unity as employees turn against one another. These are blatant indicators that toxicity is dominating the workplace.

Deal with the issue head-on. Don't put it off until later. The best answer we can offer is to identify those participating in such gossiping shenanigans and have frank conversations with them. Additionally, tell everyone on your teams and team leaders to be watchful for these symptoms of a toxic workplace. It will make it crystal apparent that you oppose such behaviour, and strong leaders always behave in this manner!

We've noticed that quite a number of our clients have experienced this. Promotion of current employees receives little consideration from managers or team leaders, who constantly seek out new hires. This creates a negative work environment where current employees feel let down by management. Along with their satisfaction levels, their drive to continue producing excellent work declines. When there are no internal promotions, it is clear that either the present staff members don't matter or aren't qualified for advancement.

Start paying close attention to the feedback provided by the staff. Ask more questions to determine whether a worker wishes to advance or take on a new responsibility. Start a training programme after that to assist these personnel in realising their full potential. Right away, you'll notice a change in their behaviour due to increased contentment!

According to 40% of employees, team leaders fail to effectively address important work-related matters. One such subject is the culture of late-night work. It makes no sense for an employee to work until midnight every day if the workday only lasts until 5 p.m. One-off late-night projects are OK, but if they become normal, it's obvious that the workplace is poisonous.

There were certain negative aspects of the WFH culture that were brought to light, including the lack of separation between work and home for employees. Since they were solely at home, many employers expected workers to work whenever they felt like it. This way of thinking must change. No matter if it is WFH or not, employment should have bounds.

Therefore, the main reasons why employees stay late into the night at work are that they have a lot of tasks to juggle and that their team leaders set unattainable expectations for them. Such a poisonous work environment has to be changed right away to prevent employee burnout and unhappiness. Speaking with managers and team leaders about how they create goals and assign work to their teams is one method to address this. Reevaluating team workloads would be the solution in this case. It is essential to ensure that each employee has a sufficient number of duties to feel challenged and make a constructive contribution to the company's success without becoming burned out.

Poor communication is a major sign of a toxic workplace environment in a corporation. The manner in which information is shared among teams and between managers and their team members affects a company's culture. Additionally, this is bad for their financial health. Because improper communication among employees reduces productivity and creativity, an unproductive work environment results. Therefore, if you observe a lack of clarity in the knowledge that your leaders and their teams possess, a communication barrier is to blame.

Launch corporate-wide initiatives and team-building exercises to bring all teams up to speed on the current state of knowledge. Breaking down any barriers to communication across teams or hierarchies is essential. Company culture, however hazy it may be, has a significant impact on a company's capacity to operate, succeed, and even survive. Typically, it begins with the senior leadership team and gradually filters down to the rest of the workforce. Companies with a strong culture are frequently bound by a shared viewpoint and a shared dedication to making things better, whether this means significantly funding DEI programmes or promoting corporate sustainability.

These businesses also make an effort to take care of their staff, who are therefore more engaged and inclined to go above and beyond for the benefit of the business.To keep it alive and well, even a strong business culture has to be nurtured. Effective human resource management, a powerful leadership vision, and long-term dedication are required for this. If neglected, the tasks that maintain a positive organisational culture can go by the wayside, allowing the characteristics of a toxic workplace to take hold. Due to the development of remote and hybrid working, which removes interactions between coworkers from a shared in-person environment where culture is more clearly recognised, culture is becoming an increasingly challenging aspect to assess.

Here are some instances of toxic workplace interactions and culture:

- Negative conduct: Those who make an effort to injure others or ensure that others suffer. People who are unable of feeling joy for others and who even minimise positive events.

- A failure to communicate: People learn about developments that affect them from others. Instead of face-to-face talks, messages and information are typically sent by email.

- Failure to listen: conversations when talking dominates over listening. rather than to comprehend, to be understood An effective listener may learn more about the ambiance or pulse of the workplace. Having more viewpoints aids in decision-making.

- Lack of knowledge and information sharing: Lack of openness is unquestionably a cause for concern. Transparency should be the governing concept, even if it is obvious that you can never tell everyone everything. It is also poisonous and, in a manner, damaging conduct to withhold knowledge and information that is recognised to be useful to others. Sharing knowledge appropriately should be seen as exemplary conduct and treated as such.

- Management inconsistencies: Managers frequently contradict themselves. possess prejudice. Embrace favouritism. are inconsistent with regard to acceptable and unacceptable conduct, performance, etc.
- Talking behind people's backs and gossiping: This type of behaviour is accepted, many people engage in it, and mistrust will pervade and become a hallmark of the workplace.
- Micro-management: Managers are directive and don't offer their staff members the freedom to come up with creative solutions to problems or to work at their best. Burnout is more likely with this type of management.
- A lack of accountability: People are not built to accept responsibility for their words and actions. constructive criticism as opposed to assistance and feedback. Playing the victim and avoiding dealing with what actually matters.
- Everyone defending their own interests: It has to do with a lack of accountability and not taking responsibility for mistakes. It's customary to cc or bcc a lot of individuals in emails as a way to ensure that the sender won't accept complete responsibility. not to keep track of stuff. being ability to direct people.
- Putting things under the rug: not taking action when something is obviously incorrect. To ignore or brush aside what is clearly incorrect in the hopes that it will be forgotten or become outdated. It is preferable to assess managers' and workers' performance based on both quantifiable job performance and attitudes and conduct. If a person does not do well on both of these aspects, they should not be viewed or thought of as a "star." Even if an employee meets the requirements for the position and performs well on the specified criteria or metrics,

poisonous conduct should never be disregarded.

How may a toxic workplace affect your health?

For some of us, the bulk of our waking hours are spent at work, which makes a toxic workplace all the more concerning. If you're unable to leave your present job, it's crucial to look out for any symptoms of job-related stress, such as concern, anxiety, dread, impatience around others, discouragement, lack of sleep, feeling unrested when you wake up, and a general sensation of tension.

A lot of individuals also struggle to separate their stress from their personal lives and bring it with them, which leads to strained relationships with their families and domestic disputes. It is possible for sentiments of hopelessness and unhappiness to originate from the vicious cycle that arises when job stress turns into home and personal stress.

A toxic or unfavourable work atmosphere might make you stressed, which causes your body to release cortisol. You may experience both physical and mental effects. People will frequently seek out little dopamine brain doses merely to feel good, which might entail munching on junk food (sugar and fast carbohydrates make us feel good temporarily) that can result in weight gain. It's critical to keep in mind that the negativity, passive-aggressive behaviour, and damaging office rumours are not a reflection on you. The first step to surviving a toxic workplace is learning to distinguish your own self-worth, values, and convictions from the everyday poisonous atmosphere.

By developing a list of the ways in which you provide value to the work and the reasons why it's crucial for you to retain professionalism, you can distinguish between the poisonous everyday environment and your personal sense of worth. Keep this list close at hand so you can immediately refer to it. Read over the reasons why you matter when the situation becomes heated and you start to question your value. This will help you refocus on the things you can control.

Another strategy to keep oneself away from toxic people is to leave work at work. Choose a landmark that is midway between work and home. Until you reach that point, give yourself permission to reflect on your day. Tell yourself it's time to switch off the negative thoughts after you've passed that stage. Using mindfulness techniques might help you reset your thinking if you're having trouble clearing your head.

It may be preferable to use your development mindset to recognise that you aren't bound by your job and that you can change the atmosphere in which you work. A genuinely poisonous work environment may be wholly harmful. Decide if it is worthwhile to remain in that unfavourable environment or whether you would want to consider other possibilities by putting your development mindset to good use.

Making pros and cons lists or having a candid conversation with those closest to you are both excellent strategies to evaluate your circumstances and determine whether your employment is worthwhile given the drawbacks. People often experience stress because they feel powerless and at the whim of other people's judgements. You may recognise that you always have options, that you control yourself and your reactions, and that you eventually get to pick whether or not to stay with the firm by changing your viewpoint, which is a result of having a development mindset.

What are the symptoms of a toxic workplace environment?

When management and staff rules and practises lead to disputes among team members and reduce productivity, the workplace is considered toxic. In other words, a poisonous workplace culture is one that offers little opportunity for employees to innovate, produce, develop, and flourish. When Eemployees frequently experience burnout. Ask yourself these three questions.

- **Are your workers frequently irritated and unproductive in their work environments?**
- **Do they frequently appear unmotivated?**
- **Do they put off doing their work till the alarm goes off at six o'clock?**

These indicate severe burnout. And a poisonous workplace environment is one of the main causes of burnout. As a result, staff productivity declines, which negatively affects business performance as a whole. Therefore, keep a careful check on your team to determine if they're exhibiting any burnout symptoms.

You must manage your staff in detail. The truth is that micromanaging won't ever be beneficial to you in the long term. Teams thrive when given the freedom to develop their ideas and make them a reality. However, if you micromanage your team, you don't give the members a secure setting in which to test out their ideas. Micromanagement can irritate workers to the point that they leave your organisation.

Another indication of a poisonous workplace culture is a company's continuously high employee turnover rate. A typical turnover is reasonable since people move occupations in search of greater prospects for advancement. But if your staff members leave your firm citing the work environment again and again, it's time to consider the following:

What is wrong with the workplace culture at your business?

The hierarchy concerns employees too much. Employees begin to feel excluded when they believe they have no voice on the team. This fuels a desire for power. Additionally, this authority is obtained through job titles in a poisonous workplace. Yes, it makes sense that workers would wish to advance naturally through the ranks.

However, in a toxic workplace environment, people would continually try to advance their position in order to feel the faux authority that comes with the title. No one may discuss toxicity in an open forum. The corporate culture just doesn't feel right in some way.

However, nobody brings up the major issue. It sounds like you?Because they don't feel comfortable at work, your workers are hesitant to discuss the culture. They could even believe that if they speak up against the toxic workplace, they won't be heard or, worse, that doing so would result in negative consequences. How should you handle a bad workplace? You can't always be surrounded by others who share your opinions.

Are you burnt out, or is the culture of your firm the issue?

You set reasonable goals for achieving work-life balance. Let's say your goal is to create a solid, well-balanced culture where emphasis is placed on employee wellbeing. If so, your business has to establish policies and procedures on work-life balance. In order to establish new limits, it may be necessary to impose official "blackout times" during which workers are not permitted to send or react to emails or messages.

Alternately, it might include establishing new standards by applauding those who disconnect rather than those who are "always on." A great example of how companies might begin to openly define new, healthier standards and norms for their employees is Google's recent "Well-being Manifesto." Reward performance, not busywork or politics.

Politics is entangled with harmful workplaces. In other words, achieving outcomes and adding value is insufficient to advance. Systems that are toxic promote incorrect behaviours, such as outward appearance, the appearance of busyness, or just fitting in with the crowd. Systems like this predispose some employees—such as those with diverse backgrounds or those who are quieter and more reserved—to failure from the outset. There is little doubt that working in an environment like this would be bad for one's mental health and lead to ongoing difficulties with turnover.

Workplace culture is a set of common values and norms that govern how people behave and interact inside a company. According to research, a toxic office environment can harm productivity. Existing cultural problems tended to be amplified by the epidemic. Burnout and fatigue symptoms might be mistaken for signs of a toxic workplace.

According to 2015 Harvard Business School research, over half of workers who encountered rudeness at work decided to exert less effort and cut their time spent there. When the epidemic struck, our attitudes toward our employment, workplaces, and, well, everything, were completely altered. When suddenly all communication was virtual and cooperation occurred from wherever we could manage it, organisations across the board were compelled to adapt their working methods on the fly, and already-existing cultural difficulties grew worse. Many businesses discovered the hard way during the COVID crisis and The Great Resignation that a positive workplace culture is essential to retaining employees and that, no matter how much you pay them, a poisonous one will drive them away.

People's lives can be significantly impacted by a positive culture. The Society for Human Resource Management reports that 74% of American workers said their organisations' principles helped them through the epidemic. Contrary to what most bosses assume, their colleagues don't think the corporate culture has improved as a result of the epidemic. How, therefore, can executives verify their perceptions of their company's culture? And how can workers determine whether they are experiencing a truly toxic work environment or a general pandemic-driven malaise?

As poisonous individuals are eliminated from your life, space and emotional energy are made available for wonderful, healthy connections.

What if your organisation exhibits one or more toxic culture indicators?

While cultural transformation won't happen over night, leaders may use technology tools to receive real-time feedback and insights into their teams and organisations, head off problems before they become serious, and, most importantly, assist their workers.

For the past few years, I've been researching what makes individuals happy at work. What I found is that the presence or absence of harmful behaviours is one aspect that significantly affects outcomes. We feel better about our employment and our coworkers in toxic-free environments, which increases our motivation to contribute. We experience more contentment, worth, and resilience. But consider this: Workplaces devoid of toxins are uncommon. There are so many toxic cultures and practises present in enterprises all around the world. I'm happy to inform you. This is not necessarily the case. Join me in putting a stop to toxic practises and fostering positive workplace environments. Make your place of employment memorable in a positive way.

Warning signals that your company culture needs repair

Negative attitudes have a self-fulfilling prophecy effect; while they are a product of culture, they also contribute to the depressing atmosphere in the workplace. Even worse, it makes it harder for everyone to get things done. 93% of workers claim that being among unfriendly coworkers makes them less productive. There is a widespread dread of failing.

No one likes to make a mistake at work. Making a mistake at work is, according to 28% of individuals, their worst concern at work. A hostile atmosphere that penalises perceived failures is very different from feeling paralysed by it, which is why many people try to prevent a fleeting face-palm moment.

Another sign of a dangerous workplace is a complete lack of psychological safety, which measures how comfortable workers are taking risks and making mistakes. The entire team suffers when members are reluctant to stretch themselves. In fact, Google discovered that psychological safety, rather than reliability, structure, meaning, or impact, had the most influence on team productivity.

Constant malfunction and confusion are present. Nobody is certain of their duties or positions. People are frequently left out of the loop, and there are many crossed wires. Members of the team hardly know which way is up. Workplaces that are toxic are havens for dysfunction and disorientation. This is due to the fact that these toxic situations frequently include a lack of trust, inadequate communication, and power struggles. Projects, meetings, and relationships regularly go awry as a result of these problems, making it harder for team members to work together.

A small amount of office gossip is typical. With 96% of respondents in a survey admitting to engaging in office gossip, most people are guilty of paying heed to rumours in some form. Toxic workplaces only surface when gossip is practised to the utmost. You've achieved a whole new level of drama if your typical workday feels like you're the star of a reality TV show. Nobody speaks out loud; instead, they choose to converse in whispers, in side-eye looks, and with passive-hostile remarks. Although it can seem unimportant, this malice has a cost. Bullying at work is linked to mental exhaustion, sadness, anxiety, and violence.

There is a constant turnover of staff, and it seems impossible to retain anyone for an extended period of time. You never know what vacant desks or unfamiliar faces you'll see at the office the next day. People fleeing in droves is a clear sign that the workplace culture is turning away employees. One in five workers who quit their employment do so because of the company's culture. Companies with intentional positive cultures have a 14% turnover rate, whereas those without intentional positive cultures have a turnover rate of 48%. Employees quit their jobs for a variety of reasons. But if it seems like everyone is leaving in droves, something is wrong with your workplace.

What attributes define a favourable working culture?

A healthy workplace culture is one that prioritises employee wellbeing, offers support at all organisational levels, and has policies in place to foster respect, trust, empathy, and support, to put it simply. Some elements of a positive workplace culture are :

- Respecting and caring for coworkers and demonstrating an interest in their wellbeing.

- Helping teammates out when they need it, being kind and sympathetic, and forgiving mistakes without assigning blame.
- Sharing inspiration with one another.
- Identifying and emphasising key ideas in the text.
- Making integrity, gratitude, respect, and trust the top priorities.

A supportive work environment enhances employee health, reduces turnover, increases employee loyalty, and promotes improved job performance, according to a number of studies. Let's look at some concrete benefits a positive workplace culture could offer a business:

Improved employee health Studies have shown that positive social connections at work are crucial for workers' health. When they have strong social connections at work, people tend to be healthier, recover from accidents more quickly, are less likely to suffer from depression, have greater cognitive capacities, and do better overall at work.

Most empirical research evaluates how compassion decreases suffering brought attention to the importance of empathy in the workplace. People may heal biologically from illness and bodily harm, as well as psychologically from loss, thanks to compassion. The idea that compassion in the workplace increases a person's loyalty to and dedication to the company while also triggering positive sentiments (such as gratitude) and reducing worry is also supported by research. By routinely demonstrating empathy, leaders may reduce staff turnover and promote employee loyalty.

Leadership studies show that when leaders go above and beyond to help, even when they don't have to, their employees respond by becoming more committed, loyal, and unselfish. A manager who is willing to go above and beyond may build a close relationship with their team, provide better results for the organisation's goals, and improve the welfare of the people they are in charge of. Studies show that this behaviour fosters positive behaviours in employees, such as taking on additional tasks, putting in extra time to help coworkers, and going above and beyond to protect the company's reputation, in addition to improving loyalty. Positive management practises can also lessen poor behaviour, including rude treatment of coworkers, disobeying supervisor orders, and failing to finish duties.

Employees who trust their manager and feel that their employment is secure are more likely to experiment and promote innovation, according to a study on the irregularities of organisational situations. Employees will slavishly follow prescribed behaviors, regardless of whether they are outdated, inappropriate for the project, or ineffective, if they fear repercussions for making mistakes or seeking assistance.

People at high-trust companies report 74% less stress, 106% more energy at work, 50% higher productivity, 13% fewer sick days, 76% more engagement, 29% more satisfaction with their lives, and 40% less burnout compared to people at low-trust companies.

In toxic work settings, there is uncertainty about roles, responsibilities, the line of command, and hierarchy. Power struggles, poor communication, or dysfunctional management might be to blame for this.

The end result is a workforce that has no idea what their responsibilities are, how to carry them out, or who to turn to for help. Gossip, cliques, passive aggression, and workplace bullying are all examples of drama. In many toxic organisations, power struggles between senior managers and those who assist them can result in interdepartmental conflict; this problem doesn't just affect non-leadership workers. As was said above in the section on establishing a culture of trust and safety, employees who are fearful have worse health outcomes and perform worse at work. The workplace is toxic when a person believes or knows that they will be disciplined for making mistakes. According to a 2019 poll on toxic workplaces that SHRM commissioned, 1 in 5 employees left their positions in the previous five years as a result of a toxic workplace culture.

Organisational culture of global giants

Amazon's organisational culture puts a constant push on workers to perform well in what they refer to as "Purposeful Darwinism." They favour creating smaller teams inside larger organisations and encouraging group decision-making with an emphasis on innovation. Amazon keeps the customer in mind and strives to preserve the standard of quality that contributed to its startup success in every division and product. Not everyone does well in a high-stress environment, and some employees report that their departure was influenced by the lack of a work-life balance. Amazon warehouse workers have voiced complaints about long hours, low pay, harsh working conditions, and exhaustion, particularly during the COVID-19 epidemic.

Google consistently wins the award for the best company culture. They let their employees work when and where they like, giving them the opportunity to be creative with their workflow. As a creative company, they encourage experimentation and encourage personnel to always keep the consumer in mind. They support open communication at all organisational levels and hold unique basic ideas. Employee development, which encourages more internal mobility and lowers turnover, is another key area of attention. DEI programmes are essential, as evidenced by reports that Google has suffered as a result of a lack of diversity.

The high-stress workplace at Tesla is completely dedicated to invention. They never hesitate to let their employees step outside of their comfort zones at work and constantly push them to attempt new things. Working in small teams and taking personal accountability seriously are highly valued in their individualistic culture, which emphasises achieving exceptional results no matter what.

However, Tesla has frequently made news owing to allegations made by former workers regarding long hours, toxic working conditions, and racism. For the last six years, Microsoft has worked to transform its culture from one of a fixed mentality to one of a developing mindset. This effort has become a crucial part of every role at the firm.

Microsoft provides many opportunities for development and advancement with a focus on teamwork and expects employees to be customer-obsessed. To create a workforce that reflects the diversity of the global population, they place a lot of focus on inclusion and diversity inside the organisation. Teamwork, empathy, and a good work-life balance are among their core values. Microsoft's chief of HR, Kathleen Hogan, won HR Executive of the Year in 2021 for her work in revitalising the company's culture.

Does workplace culture differ by country?

In fact, it does. Every nation has a distinct social culture, and the working cultures are no different. Of course, each company is unique, so you could find that a French company has a very German culture while a Japanese company has a more American-influenced culture. Let's examine some of the notable differences in work cultures between other countries, as shown by research from Hofstede's Cultural Dimensions. In Scandinavia, the emphasis is on the welfare of the workforce. 1 in 4 American workers claim to feel that way on a daily basis. The truth is that workplace toxicity is more prevalent than ever, and its effects go far beyond the typical workdays of most Americans. The data from SHRM supports what many employers observe on a daily basis: Workplace culture, contented and engaged employees, and business productivity and earnings all have a positive relationship. Everyone suffers when an organisation's culture is poisonous. Workers frequently leave their employment due to toxic conditions. Employees who work in toxic environments dread going to work, don't trust their bosses, and are more likely to see or encounter sexual harassment, age discrimination, or political affiliation prejudice. They frequently blame their supervisors for the toxicity, which cannot be ignored. Dysfunctional work cultures are caused by bad management and poisonous environments.

American businesses frequently prioritise outcomes and success and are very goal-oriented. Results are highly prized in the US since it has a very independent and competitive culture. Time off is not prioritised, and overtime is frequently anticipated. There are fewer employee safeguards and more job unpredictability. This could lead to a less collaborative and highly competitive atmosphere.

German firms prefer to employ formal titles and professional clothes and can be quite rigorous when it comes to timeliness because of their more formal work culture. While there is less socialising at work, there is also less of a demand for extra labour; instead, you are expected to come in, complete your task, and go when the clock strikes five o'clock. As a result, there is a work-life balance that is complemented by ample vacation time. Teamwork is frequently highly valued in German firms, where several subject matter experts collaborate to find solutions to issues.

The workplace culture in Japan is often more cooperative and places a strong emphasis on respect and compliance with the law. Work is frequently done in teams with a greater emphasis on the process than the outcomes, and interdependence is more prevalent than independence. There is an assumption that workers will socialise outside of work, frequently including alcohol, and that standards of politeness and hierarchy will be strictly observed. Long working hours and infrequent vacations are common expectations in both Japan and the United States.

Chinese organisations frequently favour collectivism over individuality and have tight hierarchies. Etiquette and respect are essential, especially when dealing with superiors. Although China has lately taken measures to shift away from the 9-to-5 work culture, long hours are still the norm there (working 9 a.m. to 9 p.m., six days a week). Outside of work hours, employees are expected to socialise, and personal and professional lives are frequently entwined.

Since their workweeks are shorter (on average, 36 hours) and their vacations are longer, Scandinavian employees are urged to maintain a healthy work-life balance (5 weeks of paid time off are typical). Organisations usually opt for a flat management structure and support worker independence and autonomy. What does "toxic work culture" mean? What are the symptoms of a toxic workplace environment?

First and foremost, those who are exposed to toxic environments and bad behaviour in the workplace may suffer actual, long-lasting effects. In the UK, 2 out of 5 workers say they have encountered problematic behaviour at work, such as bullying, harassment, or discrimination, and 42% say a toxic workplace culture has negatively impacted their mental health.

Two-thirds of individuals who have encountered problematic behaviour at work indicated that it has impaired their confidence and capacity to obtain new employment, and 67% of those who have experienced it have had anxiety as a direct result of workplace bullying. This resulted in 71% of them needing counselling, showing the long-term effects a toxic workplace culture can have on people. Additionally, 29% of workers in the UK have taken time off due to an event that occurred at work, such as bullying, harassment, discrimination, or sexual misconduct. More than a third of employees in the UK have felt silenced on matters that concern them in the workplace.

Negative organisational cultures inevitably fail because happy, safe, and secure employees are essential for productivity, innovation, and success. Employee morale is being damaged, productivity is declining, and many workers are being subjected to inappropriate behaviour as a result of a bad workplace culture and bad boss characteristics. In reality, 42% of UK workers have actually quit a job because of a terrible work environment. In addition, 41% of workers say that a bad work environment has affected their productivity, and 34% of workers say that they are less involved in their work. Additionally, a startling three-quarters of people have cancelled appointments because they didn't want to meet someone with whom they had a bad connection. It's hardly surprising that more than a third said they no longer trust their employer as a result of an event involving bullying, harassment, or discrimination at work. But what might businesses do to safeguard employees?

When management and staff rules and practises lead to disputes among team members and reduce productivity, the workplace is considered toxic. In other words, a poisonous workplace culture is one that offers little opportunity for employees to innovate, produce, develop, and flourish.

How to foster a culture of positivity at work?

A positive company culture is very important to job seekers. Equally, if not more important than pay, is a satisfying workplace culture. Since employees rank corporate culture as a top consideration for open positions, having a healthy workplace culture is more important than ever. While fair and competitive remuneration is important, keeping employees satisfied needs more than just a paycheck.

To foster a great work culture, give appealing benefits and bonuses to draw fresh talent and provide the proper atmosphere to keep them around for the long haul. Numerous factors that support and carry out a company's goal and vision are necessary for business success. Employees are possibly the most important component of a business' operations and expansion since they give it a face to consumers and serve as the foundation for all of its initiatives.

Most firms place high importance on attracting and keeping great people, but not all of them can compete in a market where salaries are the only factor. Fortunately, every company can strengthen its workplace culture to provide a welcoming environment that may be worth as much as or more than money. I'll examine the role that corporate culture plays in attracting and keeping top talent and offer suggestions for fostering a supportive environment for your staff.

Why corporate culture is crucial Employees are now less likely to put up with a poor work environment, even when they are paid well. You must establish and nurture a healthy workplace culture if you want to draw in and retain top talent.

Workplace culture is a major consideration for prospective workers. A significant 2019 Glassdoor study of more than 5,000 employees from the US, UK, France, and Germany revealed that 77% of them would "consider a company's culture" before applying for a position there. Another 56% indicated that for job satisfaction, a positive company culture was "more essential than money." Furthermore, 73% of respondents from four different nations indicated they "would not apply to a firm unless its beliefs coincide with their own personal values." A high turnover rate is a result of toxic workplaces. Employees today will not tolerate a hostile work environment. Workers appeared to reconsider their objectives in the midst of the Great Recession, which was brought on by the epidemic, and witnessed record employment turnover. According to the MIT Sloan study, concerns about toxic work environments far outweigh other problems as the leading cause of turnover in a variety of industries.

Employees that are younger are more inclined to change employment. According to Lever's 2022 Great Resignation Study, 66% of Gen Z employees are expected to work there for less than a year and are more than twice as likely to quit within the next month. They quit occupations in droves in search of a position that fits their needs professionally, and if necessary, they'll accept a wage drop. Retaining employees is harder than ever. After the Great Recession, it has become vital for businesses to figure out how to keep their current workforces and attract fresh talent. Employers consider their people as investments, while employees feel the same way about their employers. Companies with flexible work policies and happy employees appear to have higher retention rates and potentially attract more customers.

Have you heard?

A welcoming working environment must also foster an inclusive culture that offers a secure environment for all staff members and fosters a sense of community.

No matter how hard you try, there will always be team members who disagree with your method of operation. How, therefore, can you guarantee that you live up to their expectations while maintaining a productive workplace? Here are a few suggestions:

- Establish a culture of constructive criticism and feedback. Praise publicly while criticising privately. Make sure the criticism is constructive and motivates the employee to do better, even if it is delivered in secret. Your staff looks to you for criticism of their work and advice on how to raise their level of performance as a whole. Therefore, constructive criticism, where applicable, can help you retain your best talents.

- Avoid micromanagement and concern about production. Unproductivity does not equate to physical absence. Your crew isn't idly sitting around doing nothing just because you can't see them in person. Avoid being a victim of productivity paranoia. Trust your group and give them the freedom to operate autonomously. As was already mentioned, refrain from micromanaging at all costs. Instead, provide some precise criteria to evaluate productivity. Employees like it when they feel like they are in control of the task they are doing and when they are aware that their bosses or leaders are not micromanaging every action.

- Determine weak points and establish standards. Does your team have a weak point that prevents collaboration? Do certain members require ongoing behavioural oversight? Establish a clear code of behaviour and make sure all members adhere to it. It is your duty as a leader to effectively express the corporate rules. Make sure that everyone on the team is aware of their responsibilities. Keep in mind that creating a healthy workplace is a team effort, which starts with you.

Workplace Culture Is Important. There is widespread toxicity, which harms both firm profitability and personnel.

Growing your firm and team need a strong corporate culture. Employees who want to be challenged and involved in their work will be drawn to a culture that fosters personal and professional growth. How to create a better, more uplifting workplace culture is as follows:

Conduct performance reviews to enhance workplace culture. Although doing performance evaluations might be tedious, they have a big influence on your team's development when done wisely and carefully. Relationships may be strengthened and productivity can be increased by reviewing employees' progress and inviting their comments. A supportive and evolving corporate culture may be fostered via regular evaluations.

Use employee surveys to enhance workplace culture. Employee surveys are a proactive way for businesses to get input that may both benefit the business and show employees how important they are. By asking for employee feedback, managers and owners have the opportunity to examine their company from several angles. Everyone benefits when they take action on employee ideas.

Flexible work arrangements enhance corporate culture. Even if they are unable to boost salaries, firms may demonstrate their appreciation for employees by offering flexible scheduling alternatives. Companies with flexible work environments are more likely to attract new employees. People used to working from home and taking advantage of flexible work rules have resisted companies' strong post-pandemic "return to office" directives.

Possibilities for career advancement enhance workplace culture.Companies that promote professional development and provide a career path frequently retain their personnel. Companies that provide new hire training programmes, mentorship programmes, and promotion tracks encourage a supportive workplace atmosphere and guarantee higher rates of long-term employment.

Stress management techniques enhance workplace culture. Whether or whether they enjoy their jobs, many individuals experience stress at work often. The stress of deadlines, pressure, and multitasking can cause burnout in workers. You can help retain top employees and attract top applicants if you figure out how to establish a stress-free workplace.

Stressing your mission enhances workplace culture.People want to work for organisations they believe in, therefore it's critical to have a purpose and vision statement that align with the opinions of both current staff members and prospective hires. According to a Glassdoor poll, 66% of participants stated having a clear objective is crucial for maintaining engagement at work. Your firm will move in the path that its people are willing to follow if you make your objective clear. What other factors affect employee happiness? There are additional aspects than business culture that affect employee happiness. Here are a few more strategies to guarantee a happy staff.

Provide fair and affordable remuneration. Outside of fostering a positive workplace culture, paying workers fairly and competitively is the simplest method to keep them content. Understanding the market and the expectations of your sector offers you an advantage in retaining and expanding a team. The costs associated with employing staff are high, therefore it's crucial to find and retain the best applicants. Increase pay regularly, and wherever feasible, promote from within. Building a strong culture that increases employee engagement involves keeping your salaries competitive and anticipating the market.

Have faith in workers. At work, employees cherish being trusted. Longer-term employees ought to be able to profit from trust and respect because it usually takes time to establish trust. A culture of trust is beneficial for employing new employees. Candidates for jobs that desire that degree of confidence in their professions will be drawn to organisations where employees have autonomy and flexibility.

Provide the finest rewards attainable. Even if your compensation isn't as high as some rivals, having a strong employee benefits package that includes a paid time off (PTO) policy may go a long way toward luring new hiring and maintaining good present ones. To enhance employee well-being, give employees the tasks they like, encourage teamwork via team-building activities, and support their long-term career aspirations.

A positive workplace culture pays well.

Finding the proper individuals as businesses grow might be difficult in the current job market. Businesses must take into account a variety of structures, such as on-site, hybrid, and remote models, as well as alluring staff advantages like flexible scheduling and paid time off.Everyone wants high compensation, but there is a limit to what workers would give up to acquire it. By encouraging employee satisfaction and long-term goodwill, a healthy corporate culture may protect your organisation.

You don't start out in a new job with nothing on you. You come to the world (and your job) with all of your preconceptions, assumptions, and expectations. These are your guiding ideals, shaped by your experiences and cultural background. When these covert (and frequently detrimental) ideas show up in people's behaviour, cultures in many organisations become unstable or dysfunctional. and eventually have an impact on how people generally regard one another and their work.

While social gatherings and HR initiatives are crucial, businesses must also realise that a healthy, wellness-focused culture cannot be maintained if damaging work behaviours or conventions are tolerated. In other words, it's crucial to assess the workplace. Companies must determine if their culture supports actions that jeopardise the long-term health and wellbeing of their employees.

Leaders will be able to determine whether their workplace is problematic or promotes harmful views using this list. These indicators offer a glimpse into the underlying presumptions, convictions, or expectations that are at the root of the problem. These underlying assumptions must be refuted and replaced with healthy ideals in order to bring about long-lasting cultural transformation. It's interesting to note that any of these cultural issues might arise in a remote work environment. This serves as more evidence that workplace culture is more about intangible elements like how employees interact with one another than actual office furnishings.

Employees are concerned that disconnecting would result in unjust punishment. Excessive job stress is frequently attributed to a lack of work-life balance. Of course, it is the duty of each employee to understand how to unplug and detach from work. This is easier said than done, though. This is particularly true if everyone at work has an "always-on" or "urgency culture" mindset. With this unsaid expectation looming in the background, achieving work-life balance becomes even more challenging. Consider how it would feel if all of your coworkers—as well as your boss—were always responding to emails and instant messages, even while they were on vacation.

Although they aren't officially encouraged to, employees will feel compelled to perform to these standards if they're vying for a raise or promotion, even if it means sacrificing their mental health. These routines and behaviours must also be addressed if you are actively working to create a wholesome and balanced workplace culture. If this behaviour continues, it will surely have an effect on your workers' long-term wellbeing and the culture of your business.

A general sense of "busyness" prevails. It is common to work long hours. A recent study by the WHO found that working long hours (55 or more hours per week) results in the yearly death of hundreds of thousands of individuals. According to global research, working long hours contributed to 745,00 deaths worldwide in 2016 due to heart disease and stroke. It's a cruel fact that many firms have an overworked culture where everyone always seems to be busy.

Why does this issue persist despite the fact that we are aware of how harmful these conditions are to employees' wellbeing?

generating not just unneeded stress and fatigue but also sickness and death! Many firms have the implicit idea that putting in long hours and appearing busy leads to increased production. This idea dates back to the industrial era. The amount of time a worker spent on the factory floor during this period had a direct influence on production. Similar to the last example, no one specifically directs staff to work that much, but if it's the unwritten standard across the board, staff will feel compelled to follow suit. And the excessive hours and "busyness" culture will endure.

Once more, a culture killer might be a crowded environment that causes unneeded stress, burnout, and turnover. If executives want to create a solid, healthy culture and promote improved employee wellbeing, they will need to tear it down from the ground up. People are reluctant to speak up or be open with authority. Your workplace culture may be in peril if employees are reluctant to voice suggestions or complain openly about anything that is troubling them. A climate of fear and intimidation at work may make people reluctant to speak up. What then causes this kind of workplace environment? Implicit norms like the ones listed below may be deeply embedded in your culture and harm psychological safety at work. If your culture has an unspoken rule that "vulnerability equals weakness," employees may be reluctant to express their emotions or display behaviours that can be interpreted as "weakness," such as confessing to being overworked or stressed out and in need of a break.

If your leadership has the attitude that "employee opinions aren't important," then it's possible that you don't frequently ask your employees for their opinions. Or perhaps executives and decision-makers will just collect employee input as a formality without acting on it. Worst case scenario: Workers who raise concerns are silenced and secretly disciplined.

Employees won't feel secure or concerned enough to voice their concerns as a result of these measures. As a result, people frequently become apathetic and disengaged and won't even try to provide feedback because they know, in the end, it won't change anything. These unsafe psychological work settings foster a toxic culture that may be detrimental to employees' mental and emotional well-being. Ultimately, firms that don't actively address these crucial underlying concerns may experience a problem with excessive turnover.

Although everyone is aware of the issue, nobody is speaking about it or taking action. One of the most telltale symptoms of a cultural issue is when staff members surreptitiously talk about it; HR is aware of the situation, but no one is bringing it up. For instance, if an unusually high number of workers are taking burnout leave, but no one is discussing the most crucial factor—why it's occurring—in a nutshell, the working circumstances that led to burnout in the first place are not being addressed. This problem is also a result of the absence of psychological safety within the company. Due to the possibility of resistance or scepticism, it could be challenging for HR and managers to raise these issues with senior management. It's possible that some leaders won't even want to acknowledge the issue!

It's because a lot of leaders don't own up to their concerns about wellbeing. They delegate responsibility for developing new perks or programmes to HR, and they want employees to use these initiatives to improve their own wellbeing. But it's not the best course of action for enduring cultural transformation. "Few corporate executives ever want to concede that they are the issue, that their managers lack empathy, or that while being financially successful, their business strategy may hurt employee well-being." The obstacles preventing "complete worker wellness" from becoming the rule rather than the exception include failure-related anxiety and the difficulty of reflecting on oneself.

Consider a worker who is overworked and doing the duties of two individuals. This situation occurs much too frequently, even in workplace environments that appear to be positive. Of course, these obligations have an influence on each employee's degree of stress. But what management frequently overlooks is how these heightened demands affect the overall tone of an organisation. In other words, how coworkers interact with one another.

I'll explain. When groups or individuals are overworked, they will inevitably start to guard their precious time. This may lead to individuals engaging in constant haggling over these few supplies. The lack of resources can also result in bottlenecks that reduce efficiency and production. As a result of the frustration and exhaustion caused by these obstacles to production, this sort of work environment can cause a loss of trust and collaboration among the workforce.

Making sure that staff workloads are manageable and sustainable is essential to developing a healthy culture. but also giving them the resources they need to execute their jobs well. Employees are more likely to be in good moods, assist one another, and work together without difficulty when they have the time and resources to complete the task at hand. Therefore, productive cooperation has a net beneficial influence on employee relationships and, consequently, the overall work culture of your organisation. Making skewed decisions is a concern. The most common cause of burnout, according to a well-known Gallup poll of 7,500 full-time workers, was "unfair treatment at work." In the workplace, "unfair treatment" can refer to a variety of things. But prejudice is typically what it comes down to. Furthermore, prejudice is only an unstated presumption.

One could have unconscious prejudices or beliefs about persons of a particular race, age, gender, or background, for instance. Therefore, these prejudices will have an impact on how they behave at work. These opinions will ultimately affect who is employed, promoted, paid more, etc. Organisations that deliberately create diverse cultures are more inventive and financially successful, according to research, than those that don't. For instance: According to Mckinsey research, businesses with greater gender and racial diversity were 25% and 36% more likely to outperform those with less diversity, respectively.

On the other side, unjust treatment of employees may result from biassed decision-making and a lack of openness in the workplace. Employee connections suffer when they are dissatisfied and resentful, which hurts the culture of your business and ultimately your bottom line. The following point may surface as a result of a work environment where people feel unjustly treated. The staff is covertly cheering against one another.

An inordinate quantity of badmouthing between coworkers should be a major warning sign.It's a solid indicator that your society is experiencing some unsettling changes. This is particularly true if employees are talking negatively about one another behind one other's backs. On the other side, in a positive work atmosphere, coworkers support one another. They will trust one another, work well together, and share triumphs as a team. So how did a workplace get to be so nasty and chilly? The aforementioned problems and demands can foster an unhealthy atmosphere of competitiveness that makes workers feel like they are competing against one another instead of uniting for a shared objective.

Mentality of "always on," "vulnerability = weakness," rewarding "busyness" rather than outcomes, biassed decision-making, workload exceeding resources available.

These kinds of settings frequently have an unseen power struggle behind many encounters. Employee competition is gently promoted. People that engage in this behaviour may take credit for one another's efforts, work behind one another's backs, or spread unfavourable rumours among themselves. These all play a part in creating unhealthy corporate cultures.

Important professional decisions, including who gets promoted or gets paid more, are susceptible to prejudice.Even worse, when businesses keep their decision-making processes under wraps, it may make employees distrustful, angry, and unhappy. This unfavourable mindset has the potential to fuel social unrest. In order to manage perceptions of fairness and, ultimately, maintain your employees' happiness and prevent them from working against one another, prejudice must be controlled. Major decisions, like promotions and increases, cannot be decided unilaterally, for instance, at Google. A committee of management makes them. And for employee assessments, a similar calibration procedure is used. These actions are essential for sustaining employees' impressions of fairness and guaranteeing openness.

Give employees the tools they need to execute their tasks well.

Social gatherings alone won't be enough to create a productive workplace culture. Additionally, it involves making sure that staff members have adequate time and energy to complete their best job and collaborate well with their colleagues. For instance, you may initially save money by having one person do the duties of two. Even so, imagine the person is overworked and hence really unpleasant to deal with. Or even worse, as a result, they (and their team members) lose interest. In such instances, you can discover that you have a burnout and turnover issue, which will undoubtedly have a greater long-term impact on the bottom line of your company.

Take action on employee input. Congratulate those who speak out.How do you think employees would feel if they raised a concern with management only to have it disregarded or shut down? In order to engage with workers and create a psychologically healthy culture, it is important to pay close attention to what they have to say. It also entails showing gratitude to them for bringing about challenging transformations and acting to put things right whenever you can.

You can lessen cultural imbalances or dysfunctions by assembling teams with members who have a variety of opinions and backgrounds. However, many people are unaware that they have prejudices, let alone want to share them with others. As a result, achieving this aim may be challenging. However, it is a target that has proven to be quite beneficial for businesses. As I have discussed, research demonstrates that increasing diversity at work has a positive effect on culture and, eventually, your bottom line.

Problematic behaviors, including exclusion, rumours, deceit, intimidation, and others, spread like viruses. If you opt to ignore detrimental behaviour, you may quickly destroy your company's culture and undermine the aggregate productivity and engagement of your staff. Even Nevertheless, studies have shown that it only takes a few "bad apples" to destroy the batch. According to Harvard research, companies may save $12,500 by avoiding just one toxic hire or by immediately firing one. In other words, a single bad apple might cost your company money.

The biggest error businesses make when trying to enhance culture or avoid burnout is merely making surface improvements, like increasing social events or introducing new HR programs. Although superficial modifications are usually the simplest to adopt, they frequently have a limited lifespan since they do not address the underlying cultural problems. Sadly, creating a strong workplace culture cannot be accomplished in a single step. To build and sustain a more balanced and resilient culture, all employees—not just HR or even leaders—must seek these tiny, thoughtful improvements. The values, conventions, and expectations that guide your business may be closely examined by peeling back the layers and starting from scratch to create a strong culture.

Finding the ideas that are causing issues is the first step in replacing them with better standards and behaviors. You may progressively enhance your culture and maintain people's happiness and health in this way. Toxicity at the organisational level indicates that you need to discuss your basic beliefs. If you can relate to any of the following, you and the rest of your leadership team are probably causing toxic behaviour in the office.

You don't have clearly defined fundamental values. Your expectations for your staff are reflected in your business values. They serve as the basis for your choices and your expectations for your team members' conduct. It may be challenging to build and transmit culture without them. The frameworks offered by these publications are ideal for defining and establishing your company's values. Rather than serving as the foundation for how your business runs, your key beliefs are used as website content.

Your fundamental principles are more than just something you claim to be good at. You need to put your principles into practice. At all-company meetings at The Predictive Index, we discuss our company's core principles. We frequently discuss them in our once-a-week team meetings. We have specific Slack channels where we praise colleagues who behave in ways that are consistent with our fundamental principles. On televisions located throughout the office, we also advertise our ideals. Even our yearly bonus is determined by our basic beliefs as opposed to performance. This encourages a strong organisational focus on embracing and upholding culture every day.

It's time to reevaluate how you convey your organisation's principles if your workers are unable to list them. You must also consider how you build a culture based on those ideals. Your policies and practises don't reflect your basic principles. We frequently develop processes and procedures apart from the guiding principles of our business. It leads to misalignment. Let's imagine, for instance, that your business believes in giving its workers the freedom to handle their own issues. It will be difficult to establish the type of atmosphere and outcomes you want if your supervisors micromanage.

Energy is one of the basic values at PI. Around this idea, we built our unlimited vacation time benefit. Burnout among employees causes low morale, decreased output, and a greater turnover rate. We want our staff to have enough time to refresh in their personal lives so they can do their best work. Improved work-life balance has a favourable effect on your workers' mental health and general wellbeing, which helps your entire company. Examine your policies, practises, and even your perks. Look for areas where the standards already in place and the values held by your business may not be in alignment.

You act in a particular manner because "that's how it's always been done." As leaders, we should always seek to improve and adapt what we're doing in order to better reflect our fundamental beliefs. An annual performance review is something that most businesses carry out since it allows them to pinpoint a person's worth to the business. Performance evaluations unfortunately don't always provide the expected results. Performance management places an emphasis on how an individual is performing in comparison to his or her peers, as Dr. Joanna Wilde explains in her book "The Social Psychology of Organisations." However, this frequently results in an unhealthy culture of competition—and the resulting disengagement.

Examine what you're doing at the moment and consider how it relates to your basic principles (or not). Are these actions having the desired outcome? An essential part of sustaining a healthy workplace is realising this and making the required adjustments. You don't consider the wants and motivations of others. Understanding behaviour at the individual level is crucial.

What makes humans tick? What requirements do they have in particular? Every employee in your firm has different behavioural demands and drives. Knowing this helps you predict how various individuals will react to change. This answer might be given in either a positive or negative way. In any case, it needs to be addressed on a personal level, which again requires knowledge of what inspires and drives each person.

Additionally, it is crucial that executives and staff members from all levels of the business comprehend their own behavioural motivators and demands. The Harvard Business Review's "On Managing Yourself" is among the greatest self-help books I've read that have also advanced my career. It discusses how to combine work and life and develop your self-awareness to be more productive at work. Toxic bosses have the ability to harm the environment. As the cliché goes, terrible managers drive away good staff.

You don't coach and mentor your direct subordinates in accordance with the company's principles. To learn how to teach and mentor others is some of the finest management advice I can provide. My study on people management demonstrated that outstanding managers care about the professional and personal development of their staff members. Talk to your staff members about your company's basic beliefs when you meet with them.

- **How are they faring compared to others? With which do they require assistance?**
- **What are their individual objectives?**
- **What are their aspirations for the future?**
- **How can you help them accomplish their objectives?**

A toxic work environment can result from poisonous employees. Not every person in an organisation holds a leadership position. However, there is a chance for self-leadership and accepting personal responsibility. We at PI support the idea of "leaders at every level."

Your bosses should provide exactly the correct amount of criticism. Employees would prefer to work under a manager who gives them too much feedback, according to new research on people management. Teach managers to lean on the side of "more" if they are unsure of what the appropriate quantity looks like. The majority of managers meet with their direct reports once or twice a week, but how frequently do they use that time to provide and solicit feedback? These sessions are an excellent venue for discussing what has been working well and what needs to change. Employees should be aware of their status. Failure to provide honest feedback on a regular and timely basis can have serious consequences.

For good reason, managers are held to greater standards than individual contributors. If managers don't support the ideals of your company, employees won't be inspired to do the same. Additionally, it poisons the air in the workplace. Keep an eye out for conflicts between your management team's activities and your company's ideals. Being aware is essential to fostering a positive work environment and raising employee engagement.

In addition to fully committing to choices, it's critical to project a sense of unity. Toxic situations need to be filtered by managers.I recall wanting to be liked as a new boss. My direct reports would visit my office to vent about anything that they didn't like. Striking a balance between acknowledging their perspectives and demonstrating my commitment as a leader was difficult. especially if you disagree with the choices being made. For this reason, businesses have "conflict management" in their toolkit. When you're in charge of others, it will unavoidably come up. My development as a leader and manager has greatly benefited from these management books. Leave these accessible for loan on a bookshelf in a public space.

Managers may lament with an employee when they bring up a complaint in order to demonstrate their comprehension and empathy. But there is a more effective way to express empathy. I'm really sorry you feel that way. Managers need to learn how to say it.

What are your options?

Managers should instruct their teams to disagree and commit when workers convey their hardships to them. Additionally, when workers at all levels of the organisation have faith in it, they are free to disagree and make commitments. Jeff Bezos often discusses this subject. The Amazon Way's thirteenth principle is: "Leaders are required to politely dispute choices when they disagree, even when doing so is difficult or taxing." Leaders are tenacious and possess conviction. They don't make concessions for the sake of societal harmony. When a choice is made, they fully commit.

Employees who disagree yet don't completely support the decisions made foster a poisonous work environment. They have rights. Resentment frequently manifests as entitlement. Consider the workers who were passed over for a position or a promotion. When asked why they didn't get the promotion, they can have an entitlement issue. In actuality, somebody could not be prepared yet. Or maybe they just weren't the right match. They might discuss how they feel about the circumstance, set their ego aside, and then inquire, "What would it take for me to get there?" after talking through their feelings. Employees can become more resilient if you teach them how to react positively to failure. This will position them for success in the future.In his book "No Ego," Disengagement and a hostile workplace are the results of this. I strongly advise reading it if any of your workers struggle with feelings of entitlement or anger.

By continuing to work in a position—or at a company—that is not a good match, people can occasionally add to the poisonous environment at work. When an employee appears to be checked out, the following questions should be taken into account:

- **Is your position the ideal one for you? Does it fit with your natural interests and strengths? Does it inspire and challenge you?**
- **Do you have the best management possible? Does he or she encourage your growth on both a personal and professional level?Is your management conscious of their own needs and sensitive to them?**
- **Is the team you're on the correct one for you? Do your coworkers encourage you to develop and get better? Do you trust and engage in healthy conflict?**
- **Do the organisation's values reflect your own?**

This employee may require a modification if the response to any of those questions is no. This could entail moving someone to a new position on the same team, a new position on a different team, or their departure from the organisation. It should be commended when someone has the bravery to admit that their job or company isn't a good match and to take action as a result. They oppose changes that are being made inside your company.In the academic world, we refer to a notion termed "psychological safety" while discussing change management. This is the notion that taking interpersonal risks is safe inside your team.

In a professional setting, this may resemble your company using a new technology, and your staff members are confident stepping up and picking up the basics since they understand that it's acceptable to not be an expert the first time you utilise a new technology. Employees that are hesitant to take chances are often those who are eager to gain new abilities or adjust to change. The popular book "Organising Culture and Leadership" by Edgar Schein can assist you in understanding and enhancing psychological safety inside your company.

Your staff aren't forthright and honest with other people.We spoke about how entitlement may lead to feelings of bitterness. However, it may also result from suppressing your emotions in a certain circumstance. The foundation of effective cooperation, according to Patrick Lencioni's book "The Five Dysfunctions of a Team," is trust. Employees will be afraid of disagreement if they don't trust the individuals they work with. Conflict-averse workers don't voice their disapproval of actions or practises. Silence can encourage hostility, alienation, and bitterness. In other words, it could encourage toxic behaviour and create an unpleasant work atmosphere.

You may also conduct a background check on prospective employees to make sure they have the same values as your business. Make certain that everyone you employ for a new position fits the culture you're seeking to foster. At the end of the day, everyone of us has an impact on whether a workplace is healthy or not. If your business is not where you'd like it to be, now is the time to implement change at all levels of the business to raise employee engagement and boost working conditions. The first step in changing direction is to simply be aware of where things are, investigate why and how they came to be that way, and then do the above-mentioned actions.

Any organisation has the potential to degenerate into a poisonous one. The powerful chemical in a toxic job is in pain. We may decide whether to be trusting and open-minded about a scenario. We are choosing to suffer if we choose not to. The average CEO rating on Glassdoor is 69%, while the typical firm receives 3.4 out of 5 stars, according to Forbes. Your office may be toxic if your ratings are below these standards. Additionally, you may check out your most current Glassdoor reviews. If they're negative, it means that your culture is in trouble and that you need to take action.

Workplace culture has always been a crucial element in attracting and keeping talent since it has a significant impact on team productivity as well as individuals' daily sense of wellbeing.

All of this raises the issue of: What or who is to blame for workplace toxicity? Who needs to be held responsible? Is it the toxic management's fault? Is this just another rising discomfort brought on by fast scaling? Is it high turnover that interferes with teamwork? Each and every member of an organisation has the potential to make the workplace toxic. Business leaders, poor management, or disgruntled staff may be the sources of the toxicity. Frequently, all three occur at once. Anyone may cause toxicity, and anyone can also find a solution to the issue. We all have the option of choosing whether or not to contribute to that poison, as I have stated. We have the option of suffering or taking action to solve the issue.

Your expectations for your staff are reflected in your business values. They serve as the basis for your choices and your expectations for your team members' conduct. It may be challenging to build and transmit culture without them. Encourage reflection if your staff find it difficult to put their confidence in the group. Why don't you trust your team, you should ask? What would occur if you raised your voice?What do you fear would occur if you did?

What role does HR play in culture building ?

The workplace culture is normally the responsibility of human resources. But it's crucial to remember that toxicity will result if leadership doesn't control the implementation of the business vision and core values. HR can't do this task by itself. There are actions you may do if you work in human resources and observe that your workplace has become toxic. You can discuss developing or promoting corporate principles with your organisation's leadership. You may also give your employees the authority to own up to living according to those ideals. Alternately, you might design deliberate behaviours that uphold the established principles. Rather than serving as the foundation for how your business runs, your key beliefs are used as website content. Your fundamental principles are more than just something you claim to be good at. You need to put your principles into practise.

The culture of the workplace is normally the responsibility of human resources. But it's crucial to remember that toxicity will result if leadership doesn't control the implementation of the business vision and core values. HR can't do this task by itself. There are actions you may take if you work in human resources and observe that your workplace has become toxic. You can discuss developing or promoting corporate principles with your organisation's leadership. You may also give your employees the authority to own up to living according to those ideals.

Alternately, you might design deliberate behaviours that uphold the established principles. You may also conduct a background check on prospective employees to make sure they have the same values as your business. Make certain that everyone you employ for a new position fits the culture you're seeking to foster. At the end of the day, everyone of us has an impact on whether a workplace is healthy or not. If your business is not where you'd like it to be, now is the time to implement change at all levels of the business to raise employee engagement and boost working conditions. The first step in changing direction is to simply be aware of where things are, investigate why and how they came to be that way, and then do the above-mentioned actions.

At all-company meetings at The Predictive Index, we discuss our company's core principles. We frequently discuss them in our once-a-week team meetings. We have specific Slack channels where we praise colleagues who behave in ways that are consistent with our fundamental principles. On televisions located throughout the office, we also advertise our ideals. Even our yearly bonus is determined by our basic beliefs as opposed to performance. This encourages a strong organisational focus on embracing and upholding culture every day. Employees are unable to reference your company's ideals. Once again, the culture page of your website cannot be the home of your essential principles. How frequently do you express these values? What methods of communication are used? It's time to reevaluate how you convey your organisation's principles if your workers are unable to list them. You must also consider how you build a culture based on those ideals.

Your policies and practises don't reflect your basic principles. We frequently develop processes and procedures apart from the guiding principles of our business. It leads to misalignment. Let's imagine, for instance, that your business believes in giving its workers the freedom to handle their own issues.It will be difficult to establish the type of atmosphere and outcomes you want if your supervisors micromanage. Energy is one of the basic values at PI. Around this idea, we built our unlimited vacation time benefit. Burnout among employees causes low morale, decreased output, and a greater turnover rate. We want our staff to have enough time to refresh in their personal lives so they can do their best work. Improved work-life balance has a favourable effect on your workers' mental health and general wellbeing, which helps your entire company. Examine your policies, practises, and even your perks. Look for areas where the standards already in place and the values held by your business may not be in alignment.

As leaders, we should always seek to improve and adapt what we're doing in order to better reflect our fundamental beliefs. An annual performance review is something that most businesses carry out since it allows them to pinpoint a person's worth to the business. Performance evaluations unfortunately don't always provide the expected results.

Your bosses give inconsistent feedback. Your bosses should provide exactly the correct amount of criticism. Employees would prefer to work under a manager who gives them too much feedback, according to new research on people management. Teach managers to lean on the side of "more" if they are unsure of what the appropriate quantity looks like. The majority of managers meet with their direct reports once or twice a week, but how frequently do they use that time to provide and solicit feedback? These sessions are an excellent venue for discussing what has been working well and what needs to change. Employees should be aware of their status. Failure to provide honest feedback on a regular and timely basis can have serious consequences.

Your management doesn't adhere to your company's principles. For good reason, managers are held to greater standards than individual contributors. If managers don't support the ideals of your company, employees won't be inspired to do the same. Additionally, it poisons the air in the workplace. Keep an eye out for conflicts between your management team's activities and your company's ideals. Being aware is essential to fostering a positive work environment and raising employee engagement.

Your bosses express sympathy to the staff. Managers may lament with an employee when they bring up a complaint in order to demonstrate their comprehension and empathy. But there is a more effective way to express empathy. I'm really sorry you feel that way. Managers need to learn how to say it. What are your options? Managers should instruct their teams to disagree and commit when workers convey their hardships to them.

Additionally, when workers at all levels of the organisation have faith in it, they are free to disagree and make commitments. Jeff Bezos often discusses this subject. The Amazon Way's thirteenth principle is: "Leaders are required to politely dispute choices when they disagree, even when doing so is difficult or taxing." Leaders are tenacious and possess conviction. They don't make concessions for the sake of societal harmony. When a choice is made, they fully commit.

Effective communication is crucial in both personal and professional settings. A key element of a profitable business operation is establishing and maintaining a safe and productive work environment. However, accepting and valuing individual diversity is not always simple. As many individuals as there are, there are also various opinions. Different people have different levels of conceptual attachment. A dispute begins with a misunderstanding.

- **How at ease do you feel at your workplace?**
- **Do you know how to spot harmful behaviour?**
- **What kind of person is your toxic coworker or boss?**

Employees who disagree yet don't completely support the decisions made foster a poisonous work environment. When managers disagree with a business choice, it is clear. In addition to fully committing to choices, it's critical to project a sense of unity. Toxic situations need to be filtered by managers. I recall wanting to be liked as a new boss. My direct reports would visit my office to vent about anything that they didn't like. Striking a balance between acknowledging their perspectives and demonstrating my commitment as a leader was difficult. especially if you disagree with the choices being made. For this reason, businesses have "conflict management" in their toolkit. When you're in charge of others, it will unavoidably come up. My development as a leader and manager has greatly benefited from these management books. Leave these accessible for loan on a bookshelf in a public space.

You don't coach and mentor your direct subordinates in accordance with the company's principles. To learn how to teach and mentor others is some of the finest management advice I can provide. My study on people management demonstrated that outstanding managers care about the professional and personal development of their staff members. Talk to your staff members about your company's basic beliefs when you meet with them. How are they faring compared to others? With which do they require assistance? What are their individual objectives? What are their aspirations for the future? How can you help them accomplish their objectives?

Employee feedback is crucial, whether it comes via ethics phone lines, whistleblower protection, or other internal incident reporting. The only way to handle internal concerns without intervention or bias from managers and executives is to have a reporting system in place. Companies with toxic leadership typically don't get enough direct feedback from workers or don't have a regular, fair, and equal reporting mechanism. without a procedure for reporting. Information on incidents from employees who deal with problems on a daily basis is lacking. Unfortunately, cultural change cannot occur—at least not quickly—without these event reports. This presents a host of issues, not the least of which are prejudice, discrimination, and retribution. That's not a very nice image.

Employees who are hesitant to take chances are often those who are eager to gain new abilities or adjust to change. Your staff isn't forthright and honest with other people. We spoke about how entitlement may lead to feelings of bitterness. However, it may also result from suppressing your emotions in certain circumstances.

How to foster a happy work environment?

- Formalise or create your organisation's vision. You may bring people together by focusing on your organisation's core values or goals. It can also assist you in forming cohesive teams and hiring individuals with similar values. Naturally, not every business will have a motivating reason, and not every employee you recruit will share that belief. However, having a clearly expressed vision allows you to provide a clear image of what you do and why you exist, which may help you draw in the appropriate people and create a sense of purpose among them.
- Clearly state the company's values. This is important. Your company should be completely open and honest about its principles. Furthermore, it's critical to show how the organisation's leadership and employees uphold these principles on a regular basis. Work with people who adhere to your culture. If you hire high performers

who do not fit your cultural norms, it will have a negative impact on them. The same holds true for present workers.

- Leadership should endeavour to assist an employee in improving their attitude when they are not acting in a way that is consistent with the culture of your company. However, if it doesn't succeed, think about letting them go.

- Promote empathy, support, and trust. Leaders may foster trust by modelling it. Managers may foster a culture of trust and enjoy the rewards by being consistent, receptive to criticism, demonstrating gratitude, engaging in active listening, trusting staff to make the best decisions, and being honest (but fair).

- Connecting with individuals around you is the key to developing empathy. Give your staff advice on how to behave with empathy, such as by: observing how others are feeling; listening intently; thoughtfully probing; refraining from making assumptions or judgements; and recognising another person's sentiments even if you don't fully understand them.

- Since empathy is a taught talent rather than a set quality, many businesses have found it beneficial to provide particular training in this area. Making empathy a priority in your corporate culture will show in your workplace culture. Establish designated areas for socializing. According to Julianne Holt's 2018 Lunstad report, Fostering Social Connection in the Workplace, businesses should set aside areas for socialising and put policies in place to promote fruitful encounters. Ping-pong tables, open-concept workplaces, and social hours for employees are a few examples of social spaces. However, meaningful relationships may not always result from this sort of unstructured environment. Because of this, systematic techniques may be more successful.

- Structured tactics might include leadership development programmes, setting up employee mentor-mentee connections, and promoting relationship diversity in both corporate positions and cultural contexts. These initiatives shouldn't, however, be carried out after work hours. Both maintaining a work-life balance and encouraging employees' individualised social networks are crucial.

- Leaders should consistently demonstrate their dedication to their team.This may be done by offering assistance with career advancement or moving up in rank, showing flexibility during times of internal conflict, or even lowering their pay to keep their jobs. Employee loyalty will rise and improve work culture when they can perceive their leader's commitment to them.

- When there is frequent, open communication between managers and employees, it may improve anything from weekly check-in messages to yearly appraisals. Create a culture that values communication and demonstrate to your staff through your actions that you will do your utmost to assist them if they come to you with an issue. It's crucial to strike a balance between this and giving staff members the freedom to come up with solutions and take initiative.Your team will quickly adopt the same qualities if you foster a friendly, nonjudgmental, and solution-focused atmosphere.

- Establish explicit guidelines for sick days, especially those for mental health. Your company should promote self-care among its staff members. Make sure you include mental health care as a legitimate reason to utilise sick days in any rules you create that address the significance of taking time off when required.

- Offer assistance with both physical and emotional health. By forming alliances with fitness centres or retailers of sporting goods, organising internal sporting events, or providing entry fees for sporting competitions like marathons, a business might seek to make healthy activities more accessible for its employees.To administer flu vaccinations, it is possible to arrange internal immunisation efforts. Some businesses collaborate with mental health treatment providers to provide service discounts.

- Have specified processes and open channels of communication. Documents outlining the procedure for HR complaints and dispute resolution should be made available to all workers, together with details on benefits, pay, vacations, relocation, and incentives. Each of these often discussed subjects must to be explained in detail, and staff members ought to be aware of who to contact in the event of a problem or query.

- Employees should focus their own growth.Employees should get ongoing training from the company in soft skills like leadership, communication, problem-solving, and creativity in addition to hard skills directly connected to their roles. Through their decisions and actions, leadership, management, and HR should demonstrate their dedication to the company and its core principles. This is essentially setting an example. Employees are fast to pick up on leadership that doesn't live the ideals they teach, and if they don't see their leadership modelling those values, they are less inclined to do so themselves.

- The tone is established by leaders, for better or worse.Simply said, it is always the duty of corporate executives to change a poisonous work environment. Whether a certain leader was responsible for the poisonous culture or not is unimportant. Employees follow the guidelines set by their bosses and adhere to them. Unavoidably, poor management will result in a bad working culture.

- One of the characteristics of a positive workplace culture is accountability, or the need to explain and take responsibility for one's own conduct. A toxic culture penalises people for accepting responsibility for minor, avoidable errors and encourages overcompensation and blaming. Honesty is rewarded in a really healthy workplace culture, and people are given freedom to develop while also being held accountable for their errors.

- Importantly, this responsibility needs to exist at every level of the company.For an accountability system to be effective, employees must buy into it, and if they feel that their supervisors are not likewise held to high standards, they will lose trust in the system.

- The tone of the workplace is defined by the employers, but every small contact by the employees reinforces that tone. Leaders may change a poisonous workplace culture by fostering education and self-improvement as well as pushing themselves to better standards.

- Employee development at all levels of staff promotes a positive, welcoming workplace culture. It also establishes unambiguous standards for worker conduct. Don't wait any longer to establish a zero-tolerance policy for sexual harassment, racism, and verbal abuse if you don't already have one.

- Not everything can be fixed by human resources. However, regardless of the size of the company, having an HR representative on staff demonstrates the employer's dedication to treating all of its employees equally, fairly, and with respect. Something is better than nothing, even if all you can afford is one HR employee or a part-time HR representative on call. Human resources specialists give unique insights into issues that may not always be clear to an organisation's management since they are educated to spot and handle toxic work cultures.

- Does your company have a plan for internal communications? Do you have a strategy in place to follow through on your promises to your staff to support anti-racist causes and take significant action? You cannot expect real change inside your business without open, honest communication and a habit of effective action. To ensure that everyone is in agreement with conduct and behaviour norms, use your communication tools. Clear communication is essential if you want to foster an atmosphere where employees are held to higher standards of accountability.

- Despite the fact that SMBs are more likely to encounter certain signs of a toxic workplace, they are not the only ones. Large corporations also have unhealthy work environments. SMBs suffer toxic culture in various ways, and they also have diverse possibilities to change that culture. In the appropriate conditions, many of the elements that might lead to toxic cultures in small firms can also be assets. When it comes to tackling the poisonous workplace culture that research indicates is pervasive in today's workplaces, small and medium-sized enterprises have particular difficulties. However, there are specific actions that leaders may take to eliminate toxic workplace norms and reestablish a work environment that values respect for one another, decency, and morality.

- Leaders must put the safety and wellness of their employees at the top of their agenda in order to prevent toxic cultures and problematic behaviours from negatively affecting the individuals at the centre of these situations. In addition to having a terrible effect on the victims, these problems frequently spread to external stakeholders, harming the organisation's reputation and eventually its financial health.

- Numerous of these occurrences might have been prevented, and businesses should use preventative measures to reduce the danger to their employees by safeguarding them. The research showed that even though the percentages varied across industries from one-third to one-in-five, many employees resisted reporting bullying out of fear of the consequences. However, the overwhelming majority of respondents across all examined industries claimed they would be significantly more inclined to report a case of bullying or harassment if their place of employment offered an anonymous reporting platform.

- Employees who report bullying or harassment anonymously may feel more empowered to do so without having to consider any potential obstacles.The security this can offer can be the difference between reporting abuse or harassment and opting to endure it in quiet. Additionally, it can give employers vital information on the cultures and behaviours that are present in their workplace, enabling them to identify any potentially detrimental tendencies and take the necessary action.

- There is no time to waste if toxic cultural aspects have been found in your organisation. Starting small makes sense since harmful workplace behaviours may be complicated and ubiquitous. You can start making life at work easier for employees, supervisors, and everyone else even if you don't instantly solve the underlying issue. To accomplish this, for example: You may start to build trust through transparency by promoting open dialogue about the present culture among staff and management.

- It's crucial to offer a high quality of life outside of work if your employees are suffering in a toxic work environment. Instead of fostering presenteeism, you may do this by encouraging employees to use their paid time off. Making and declaring your commitment to positive change, as well as emphasising that management's door is always open, may appear corny, but it's a step in the right direction.

- Are you aware of the types of employee experiences that contribute to a toxic work environment? You may improve trust and communication while also getting a better handle on the issue by accepting, acknowledging, and acting upon candid employee input. By providing your staff with training and development opportunities that complement their professional objectives, you can show them you care about their future and are committed to them. Help them see their future, whether it's in your business or somewhere else. You could even discover that it has a favourable impact on staff retention.

- Ensure that you are clear on the values of your business. Your company's values should be evident in daily operations, and employees should be aware of them.Making sure that workers feel heard inside the organisation through cooperation and communication. Specify your expectations and share them frequently. Employees should be aware of the expectations about behaviour and the standards.

- Always keep in mind that a positive company culture begins at the top. You set the tone for the rest of the firm as the boss. Your staff is more likely to act professionally and with respect if you do. A far better workplace culture will result from treating your staff with respect and setting a good example. Above all, pay attention to what your staff has to say and take action on it. One of the most important resources at your disposal is experience data from your employees, which can be used to encourage innovation, improve work-life balance, retain talent, and maintain a strong culture.

- Finally, foster an atmosphere where workers feel comfortable sharing their opinions, even when they differ from the general consensus. This is crucial for the innovation process, the employee experience, and for identifying times when workers are feeling overburdened.

No matter the size or industry, all businesses, regardless of size or sector, should place the utmost focus on fostering a people-centric workplace culture and dealing with undesirable behaviour. It has been repeatedly demonstrated that businesses that prioritise a pleasant employee experience and concentrate on fostering welcoming, inclusive, and supportive work cultures prosper and achieve greater levels of success. So, why do some organisations continue to struggle? Problematic workplace cultures can harm both employees who are directly affected by the behaviour and those who are simply observers.

Workplaces where bullying and harassment are encouraged experience high levels of attrition, causing organisations with a pervasive unfavourable culture to lose top talent. This opinion frequently reaches external stakeholders and has an effect on the organisation's reputation. Problematic workplace cultures can harm both individuals who are immediately affected by the behaviour and those who are just watching it for a long time. Prioritising a friendly, upbeat culture is crucial for a forward-thinking, contemporary work environment, in addition to fostering healthy mental health. It's time for leaders to move this positively.

You must offer proof since the references you provide inquire about values. You are needed to offer proof, answer questions on values in the references you provide, and you could even be asked to do a case study in which the values will be evaluated. Profit and sales are only a minor portion of the discussion when performance assessments are held at the end of the year. Because they are aware that the company's values are the thread that binds everything together and, ultimately, generates money, leaders concentrate on them.

Simply put, a workplace or culture is toxic if it negatively affects your quality of life. Your life is disrupted by the toxic work environment, and these disruptions begin with your physical health and finish with emotional harm.

CHAPTER THREE

The Critical Role of Leaders in Managing Toxic Workplace Situations

"Leaders shouldn't be the source of poisonous workplace environments, yet they are far too frequently."

The majority of leadership articles highlight effective leadership. This study focuses on the exact opposite: a scenario in which a person with maladaptive tendencies becomes a leader and creates a harmful, poisonous society. The influence of the person on the department and the organisation is summarised below, along with suggestions for how to handle such a person.

These poisonous leaders—who are they? What impact do they have on the company? How do they prosper in the workplace of today? Is there a cure for this?

"These are the characteristics of bullshit individuals; they will blur your imagination, take your endowments for a piece of junk, make you silly, and most essential, you need to throw them in the recycle bin."

Recent abuses of power in the business, ecclesiastical, and political spheres have rekindled interest in the shadow side of leadership. This chapter illuminates a perilous form of dark leadership known as "toxic leadership." Due to the lack of a thorough distinction between "toxic" leadership and its associated phenomena, this chapter tackles the ambiguities and specifies the characteristics, method, causes, and effects of "toxic" leadership. To make nomological differences between various constructions of dark leadership, it examines, synthesises, and integrates the current literature on toxic leadership. It then administers stimulants as well as behavioural symptoms of toxic leadership. For a sustainable company, a few modern fallacies and detoxification techniques are presented to counteract toxicity in a leader. The chapter's objective is to pique my readers' interest, strengthen their worldview, and provide fresh perspectives in order to enlighten them by offering advice and raising awareness of toxic leadership.

Bullying may happen when leaders encourage exclusive behavior. The maltreatment of one or more employees by another employee is known as "workplace bullying." Examples can include not asking specific individuals to a work happy hour, continually giving someone uninteresting work, unfairly adjusting deadlines, or arbitrarily refusing somebody access to particular applications.

If you witness this occurring or learn about complaints, always speak with the offender immediately. Think about holding group trainings on workplace norms and bullying prevention techniques. This will offer your staff more flexibility to alert you to this behaviour so you can put a stop to it right away.

Leaders who are toxic won't confront staff members who are disrespecting the company's culture. Or perhaps they are simply ignorant and naive. In any case, keeping an eye out for this behaviour will allow you to spot a leader who is out of alignment.

Pull them aside when you find this happening and let them know what you have observed. If they are not aware, politely alert them to their conduct. If they are aware, find out why they have been allowing things to deteriorate and come up with solutions on how to deal with the staff and resolve problems before they worsen. Leaders may feel unprepared to face a situation and want assistance with dispute resolution.

A lot of workplaces also experience bullying to some extent. According to a survey conducted by a significant recruiting business, 39% of employees and 51% of managers harassed respondents at work. The phrase "a set of planned and deliberate actions and deeds of a leader that disrupt the effective running of the organisation and are meant to manoeuvre, deceive, frighten, and humiliate people with the aim of personal benefits" is a working definition of toxic leadership.

There are toxic leaders in every industry in the world, including the healthcare sector. There is evidence that anywhere from 20% to 30% of leaders are toxic. In a survey of 400 CEOs, 39% of whom were in the healthcare industry, over 95% said they had come across harmful traits in coworkers. Toxic leadership may affect any setting related to healthcare or the medical field. Toxic leadership behaviours in nurse managers were found to be strongly associated with nurse-reported adverse events, including complaints, verbal abuse of patients and their families, patient falls, infections associated with healthcare, errors in administering medication, and decreased quality of care.

Bad leadership may be present in a toxic workplace. This is quite a large one. The adage "You don't leave a job, you leave a lousy boss" is well known for a reason. Poor leadership has the potential to permeate a whole organisation, and it frequently does. We described eleven different problematic boss types and provided handling advice, but here's the thing: A poor boss can occasionally be the result of another bad boss, and so on. This generational ladder of bad leadership is what, you guessed it, makes the workplace as a whole so poisonous.

The twenty-first century has been marred by a lengthy list of heinous frauds in business, politics, religion, and other areas that may be linked to the decisions taken by ambitious people in positions of power. Victims in these situations question if the failures were deliberate or the result of inept, egotistical, and careless leaders, casting doubt on the very intent and substance of the leaders. Since the beginning of society and organisations, toxic leadership has permeated both. We have all encountered choking circumstances in our work lives that have caused tension and anxiety and left us feeling poor about ourselves. Then we look for causes for our issues, and in the end, circumstances and the workplace environment share some of the responsibility. But wait—is it really only the outcome of a toxic workplace environment? Perhaps toxic leaders have imprisoned us in a bad situation because of their personality and leadership style, leaving us worse off than when they discovered us. They are poisonous and detrimental to the organisations' very core.

A toxic leader has the appearance of a negative ninja who enjoys making everything and everyone else bad. Such managers constantly look for methods to emphasise the negative aspects of any situation or undertaking, which lowers employee morale and enthusiasm. When evaluating their total performance, they place significantly more weight on counterproductive performance than on other successful performance. The marginalisation of workers due to unjustified reasons or emotions of resentment against individuals who have reached higher levels of critical thinking and are seen as threats to those in positions of authority is one of the most harmful forms of abuse. Toxic leadership is a logical tactic for portraying oneself as a winner if work is seen of as a zero-sum game with winners and losers. Toxic leadership, on the other hand, benefits the leader at the price of the organisation if the success of the organisation depends on long-term collaborative work.

Bad managers assume many different roles. It's possible that your supervisor micromanages you, continually correcting you, undermining your choices, and eventually preventing you from carrying out your duties. You can have a boss who plays the "blame game" and is quick to place blame elsewhere. If you're lucky, you may get the "No Respect" employer, who emails you at all hours, consistently misspells your name, and probably has no idea what you do.

That ecosystem was poisoned by what? According to a recent survey by a workforce consulting organisation, 56% of employees put up with a toxic boss and his poisonous habits, which create a hazardous workplace. According to another study, the top echelons of the business world contain about one in five psychopaths as managers. This alarming statistic undoubtedly illustrates the poison issue that permeates corporate hallways and slowly erodes employees' motivation, self-esteem, and morale. There are a tonne of cover stories in the media about business scandals or political frauds that name the politicians who betrayed the public's confidence.

Let's start with the brief instance of Mr. Murthi, an executive director responsible for revenue breeding at an IT company. He was not an easy person to work with. Despite receiving numerous accolades and recognitions for his superior technical abilities and industry expertise, his erratic behaviour and climate of dread irritated many people. Mr. Murthi was deceitful, immoral, prone to irrational outbursts, and harshly critical of practically everything done by others. He refused to give teams credit and was constantly engaged in a quest for revenge, which made others follow his orders. This may sound familiar to you. Fasten your seatbelt and prepare to go on an exploration of this deadly style of leadership; be aware that you may discover many situational connections within the literature. Many of us are familiar with these circumstances, either directly or indirectly. We continue to puzzle over how we got into this situation and how we misjudged our leader's leadership style.

Any environment where workers do not feel secure, supported, or heard is the lowest common denominator of a toxic workplace. Employers appreciate business culture more than ever before, and having a great work environment is a key factor in job satisfaction.

You have probably worked somewhere unpleasant at some point in your life if you are like 99% of people. Maybe you're employed there right now. It is time for a hero to emerge and take action against a corrupt system that is deliberately harming the lives of people. You are that hero!

We will become more conscious of our own unhealthy leadership inclinations as a result of the voyage. Each scenario contains self-reflective tasks to help us consider what constitutes toxic behaviour, its effects, and how we have behaved in a similar circumstance in the past. Understanding how to truly act as a leader and prioritise what you want to concentrate on for you and your team starts with this.

The toxic concepts that are currently the default setting for teams and their leaders are out of date and unimportant in the contemporary marketplace. Literally, the current situation is killing people. Suicide rates among those on bad teams with weak leadership are shocking. Everyone deserves outstanding leadership, but the antiquated methods of team building and leadership that were employed throughout the industrial revolution cannot create a life-giving atmosphere quickly enough to save lives.

Our sceptical minds would inquire about the traits and actions of toxic leaders as soon as we were able to identify and distinguish the concept of toxic leadership. The negative traits of toxic leadership are shared by many dark leaders. Even if the majority of their behaviours are consistent with those of a toxic leader, they do have one notable exception: they are outstanding masqueraders who expertly conceal their malicious intentions. He is a wolf in sheep's clothing who, delightfully, violates fundamental human rights by carefully recasting harmful ambitions as admirable goals. You may find him to be of great assistance.

Understanding these characteristics of toxic leaders may help you identify some of the causes of your stressful work environment.

"If an unfavourable viewer is staring at you with an ugly devilish eye, find a way to pull out his eyes, or better yet, defend your excellent reputation."

What can you still do if your job is poisonous because of people who want to climb the corporate ladder and lousy leaders? According to a recent poll, 73% of employees acknowledge having had an unpleasant work experience as a result of working under a toxic boss. Toxic bosses like being confrontational with their staff members, criticising them, placing blame on them, and attempting to frighten them. Their every activity is motivated by self-interest. They never give up putting their own interests—and, worst of all, those of their followers—before the organisation's goals and objectives. Aggression against the personalities and skills of one's employees is a sign of toxic leadership.

If a leader seriously and permanently harms their subordinates, they are deemed toxic. Research showed that, regrettably, some leaders let their feelings at the time dictate the tone of their workplace. Ethics failure, incompetence, and neuroticism are just a few of the traits that are frequently present in such leaders. A study also found that toxic leadership has a wide range of negative effects on both teaching and learning in schools. These include the stakeholders' terrible working relationships, which led to a host of detrimental outcomes.

- **Have you ever been forced to perform useless tasks? Have you seen a drab coworkers advance in the company?**
- **Have you witnessed being remain stationary in the same place forever?**

Nisha is a former employee who witnessed firsthand the consequences of a hostile work environment. Nisha, who was determined to aid others in navigating comparable circumstances, penned a manual on how to endure and flourish in a terrible work environment. Nisha details her personal experience of working in a toxic environment as well as the measures she took to locate a healthier, more fulfilling job. She also provides helpful suggestions and methods for handling toxic coworkers, controlling stress, and finding ways to remain upbeat and motivated in the face of adversity. Nisha aspires to inspire people via her writing to take responsibility for their own health and discover the resources they require to succeed at work.

How can you tell whether the workplace at your company is toxic? Do you have frightening worker turnover rates? Do you or any of your employees dread going to work? Your most precious resource is your workforce. They will flee if they don't feel valued or treated badly. Toxic environments are the number one reason people are leaving their jobs right now because of the Great Resignation!

Judgment is not the goal of this path toward self-awareness. Again, we are all guilty occasionally. Recognising it and making a decision to take action are what give you power.

Have you ever been led by a toxic person? You probably smiled and nodded after reading that query. Everybody has! How many of your present and previous workers look at you when they are asked the same question, then? I'm sure I can think of a few names.

We've all finished. It is a sympathetic, yet lighthearted, examination of the part each of us plays in fostering and maintaining a poisonous workplace. Whether we mean to or not, the amount of toxicity and dysfunction in our workplaces is influenced by the decisions we make. These decisions may either increase or decrease toxicity and dysfunction.

Why do some leaders succeed in creating unified, productive workplace cultures that surpass those of their peers while others create underperforming organisations plagued by negative traits like backstabbing, credit-taking, and burnout?

They gave their teams a sense of being seen, heard, valued, and supported; thus, their teams produced higher outcomes. Even though starting these dialogues during one-on-ones can be challenging and frequently requires a lot of guts, they are crucial for every new or prospective leader.

While keeping an eye on what their teams need to accomplish their wider team goals, managers should also pause and consider what they themselves need to do so. They should also become aware of the worries and anxieties of their group and develop the confidence to discuss their own. The majority of individuals desire success, knowledge, a sense of service, etc. However, if carried too far, any of these fundamental drivers might backfire. When managers understand what employees actually want, they may inspire workers, but they must watch out that they don't receive too much of a good thing.

Managers who are only concerned with the tasks at hand risk asking employees to do duties that are outside of their areas of expertise. It's wonderful to push people to improve, but it's not healthy to set them up for failure. Recognise people's strengths and utilise them appropriately by placing them in appropriate roles. The productivity that only results from people employing their greatest abilities will rise as a result of this.

Employee retention and motivation are more likely to occur when managers relate their team members' work to the larger goals and objectives of the business. Managers may help their staff put the function they perform in a bigger context and feel less like an anonymous gear in the machine by showing interest and having these dialogues.

I would underline the shift in effective leadership from an emphasis on power to a reliance on trust when juxtaposing old and contemporary leadership. Risk is necessary for learning to occur. Without trust, taking chances becomes uncommon. Because they are lacking in interpersonal abilities and emotional intelligence, toxic leaders can occasionally be self-destructive.

Unbelievably, they are also hoarders. In order to retain tight-lipped control over their subordinates, they dig out knowledge, resources, and assignments for them. Their operating method is a culture of dread. Threatening the subordinates with bad outcomes may appear appealing at times as a simple, straightforward method of accomplishing the task, but it poisons the workplace environment. A poisonous leader's go-to word in the dictionary is authoritarianism. They don't care about a subordinate's education or team building; instead, they disparage them at every chance they have and behave as if the subordinate is nothing more than a tool to be used. Forget considering the subordinate's perspective; even their agreement with official choices is meaningless since they must obey the instructions of a poisonous boss. They enjoy micromanaging.

The body of available research underscores a key characteristic of toxic leadership: the tendency for leadership studies to place more emphasis on specific leaders than on the process by which followers and surroundings are taken into account. Although we must look at individual causes before coming up with a remedy for organisational toxicity, these behaviours do not occur in a vacuum. The historical behaviour of toxic leaders reveals that these traits did not emerge overnight; rather, they developed gradually.

You must have now grasped the distinction between a poisonous leader and a toxic leader. Remind yourself that a toxic leader is someone with negative personality qualities by using the refresh button. A toxic leader is someone with a dark, destructive disposition, but other requirements must also be satisfied for toxic leadership to flourish. Not only do dysfunctional leader actions result in negative organisational consequences, but so do gullible followers and the supportive environment in which they engage. It is known as a "poison triangle."

The toxic triangle's three elements and how they interact with one another define the level of toxicity in an organisation. Perceived threats to status, authority, and controls are one of the frequent causes of toxic leadership that have been linked to the rise of such behaviours in susceptible leaders. For some leaders, the desire to rise to positions of influence might even turn into an addiction. Their own personal goals take precedence over the organisation's long-term welfare. Leaders who lack patience and are perpetually tense in the office may also produce toxicity. These managers establish a pattern of yelling, uncontrolled conduct, shouting, harsh language, publicly demeaning staff, and unrealistic expectations.

It is also possible to blame unchallenged superiority for the poisonous behaviour that certain dogmatic leaders exhibit as they go up the corporate power structure. The effect and influence of their actions increase with their ascent in rank. In positions of such authority, people's inflated egos render them unpredictable and unpleasant to the opinions and ideas of others. This, coupled with a stubborn narcissistic mentality, may cause them to be oblivious to their own attitude and the conduct that causes dysfunction in people around them.

The chokepoint Competitive business hallways may occasionally become a hazardous breeding environment. There aren't many unethical leadership behaviours that interfere with a leader's ability to sustain high-performing teams and efficiently produce rising bottom lines for firms. Leaders are under pressure to implement a successful change in the organisation.

Researchers have demonstrated that a highly competitive environment has a tendency to increase stakeholder pressure on dishonest behaviour and to justify the appearance of the shadowy side of leadership. Through unproductive policies and practises like unrealistic objectives, excessive internal competitiveness, and cultures that promote blame-game behaviour, organisations may also turn into breeding grounds for toxic conduct. As a result, toxic leaders put a lot of pressure on others around them to be creative, imaginative, enthusiastic, and independent in order to further their own interests.

Difficult individuals disregard logic and the law. Some people seem blissfully unaware of the harm they cause to those around them, while others seem to find pleasure in causing commotion and setting other people off. In any case, they add needless complexity, conflict, and—worst of all—stress, forcing some people to engage in unproductive behaviour while forcing others to submit to immoral, spiteful behaviour.

Calculating the damage to the organisation's culture is a logical technique to determine the extent of toxic behaviour in the workplace. According to statistics, toxic leadership caused a 48% drop in work effort and a 38% drop in work quality. Another poll conducted in 2017 uncovered some alarming data, including 73% of turnover attributed to a toxic CEO.

Through several studies, it has been repeatedly confirmed that while the negative consequences of toxicity may or may not become apparent right away, they steadily broaden over time, threatening the organisation's basic structure. Such leaders frequently rank at the top of the charismatic scale, making it challenging to establish their toxicity, which gradually manifests over time. Because perceived toxicity varies from person to person, a toxic leader for one person could be a hero for another.

Through several research studies in the past, the truth about the physical and psychological harm caused by toxic leadership has been demonstrated both practically and conceptually. The consequences at both the subordinate and organisational levels are estimated by presenting numbers of unproductive work behaviour and employee deviation operating under the auspices of toxic supervisors. Toxic leaders feed the pessimism that permeates an organisation. Autocratic bosses who prioritise self-promotion and pleasing upper-level management have a negative impact on corporate culture and human resources. The sycophant style of management and leadership is a cunning ruse that does significant harm to the organisation's performance and morale.

An increase in unproductive work behaviour, showing up late for work, quitting their jobs, or being transferred are all consequences of toxic leadership, according to a research study. Few studies have examined the wide range of negative effects of toxic leadership. At a personal level, the impacts are more pronounced and substantial. Reduced self-esteem and self-insight are at the top of the list because they cause people to question their own talents and produce feelings of poor self-worth. As a result, certain psychological reactions are fairly visible, such as feeling threatened, distressed, or betrayed, feeling mistreated and having lesser motivation, as well as feeling helpless and burned out, which forces them to voluntarily resign.

According to several surveys, stress and issues associated with it, such as heart disease, account for around 90% of all hospital visits. If stress is consistently experienced, dangerous diseases like cancer may also develop. The so-called leader with no actual leadership characteristics would be the major cause of the disaster if such poisonous conduct spreads throughout the organisation through the culture.

An ineffective leader will take advantage of the instability and terror in the culture to intimidate and manipulate his team members. Such fake pirates are helped by this kind of sadistic mindset to support their ignorance of expert advice, which makes their subordinates dependent on them for all professional solutions and guidance.

The organisation is in serious difficulty as a result of this control strategy. One of the negative effects of a toxic leader on people is a sense of helplessness. Other negative effects include a lack of opportunity for innovation, a lack of professional sovereignty, diminished efficiency, lower job satisfaction, and job insecurity leading to a variety of psychological and emotional issues, such as anxiety, depression, and frustration. This may not always be peaceful or alone. The tit-for-tat strategy may convince the victimised worker to respond to their supervisor's exploitation by acting aggressively and inadvertently at work.

Senior executives have the ability to create a work environment in which individuals can grow and contribute their best efforts or a toxic environment in which no one is satisfied. Executives' mental health has a bearing on how they use their authority. Employees are often free to concentrate on doing their work properly because sound, stable CEOs create organisations where the rules make sense. However, if the boss is psychologically unstable, his or her illnesses will show in the organisation's procedures and structure as well as in business goals, ideas, interactions, and even interpersonal relationships. As an executive coach, I occasionally see executives who are battling mental demons. In an effort to understand and help some of these employers, I've seated them on the sofa. The diseases I've encountered and how I've assisted people in overcoming them are described in the pages that follow.

Notably, individual cases of depression are not included in these diseases. We all experience depression since it is a component of the human condition. It doesn't call for a specific coaching intervention when it's only mildly evident. And it frequently forms a portion of the disorders I'll discuss here, both when they're acute and when they're chronic.

We are frequently a little bit of this and a little bit of that; hardly everyone cleanly fits into one of the categories I describe. However, a surprising proportion of senior executives actually suffer from a personality disorder of some type. while the majority of managers are not mentally ill. Even with CEOs who are emotionally in reasonably good shape, you almost always encounter some of the traits listed below, which need to be dealt with similarly (though not necessarily accompanied by medication and formal therapy).

What qualities distinguish a successful leader?

An inspiring leader may see possibilities in chaos and motivate followers to follow them towards a brighter future. In light of the state of the globe today, this has never been more crucial. Working remotely and conquering new challenges must be paired with managing staff productivity and performance, all while preserving psychological well-being, upbeat morale, and a robust company culture. On the other side, an ineffective leader abandons you to handle everything on your own or is too preoccupied putting out fires to be able to lead.

A disruptive or poisonous boss, however, is worse than that. These people simply consider opportunities for self-improvement, taking advantage of others to increase their own benefit without giving any thought to the possible emotional harm they may create. It is obvious that toxic leadership behaviour must be avoided at all costs. What causes such poor leadership behavior? And how can you recognise them and keep from selecting this kind of leader? It's crucial to note right away that everyone has quirks that irritate those around them. It seems natural that we would be hostile to others who behave differently from us given our distinctive ways of acting, thinking, and reacting in a range of situations. Our DNA encodes our traits, which are also shaped by the environment in which we were raised. However, poisonous leadership traits go beyond simple personality conflicts.

Instead of displaying regular behaviour patterns, these people instead display significant aberrations that are fueled by the brain's more primal regions, including fear. Responses to these patterns turn harmful when they become ingrained. For instance, the ego might store a notion of being diminished by significant caretakers if a person had received excessive criticism throughout their early development. In exchange, they would feel even more strongly that avoiding criticism is essential to their existence. This might easily result in an obsession with feeling better than others to allay the anxiety of being inferior.

When they are unable to overtly react against the boss, employees frequently vent their frustration on the company, their subordinates, and their coworkers. The organisation is ultimately harmed as a result of the impact of the power imbalance and their incapacity to confront the abuser.

Although they have no choice but to follow his directions or die from the system, toxic leaders urge individuals to take sides. Employees are required to "join his army or be ready to face it" since they control the system. People therefore make exit plans, which increases the turnover rate in businesses. This raises the cost of hiring and training new employees for businesses. not to mention the mysterious skill shortage they experience.

However, there is also bad news for the organisation regarding the remaining intrepid hovers. Those people are either conformists or conspirators who might not be devoted to the success of the organisation and its aims. The effects of toxic leadership are similar to those of an institutional cancer that has a strong propensity to spread, leaving devastation, poison, and scars in its wake. It is now well accepted that toxic leadership has a negative impact that extends much beyond the employees, projects, and organisations. It seeps deeply into society, endangering the development of an advanced country.

Healthy leaders typically have a few bothersome tendencies. But when you go further, you'll find two key differences that distinguish great leaders from destructive ones. Optimal leaders develop a mentality that demonstrates concern for how one affects others and a willingness to learn, listen, and exercise the will and character to change. Have good intentions for other people and endeavour to further the goals and interests of the organisation they represent. As opposed to this, toxic leaders include those who are:

- They are uncoachable because they have a strict worldview that suggests they don't care about how their actions affect other people and will use their power to persuade subordinates to do as they like. The best way to sum up their motto would be "I am who I am, so deal with it."
- They are acting with a covert ulterior goal to benefit themselves at the expense of others, the mission, or the business.
- Keep this in mind as we examine the four signs of toxic leaders in detail. Is the leader well-intentioned and eager to improve? If so, they probably want to help their company as much as they can, even if that means picking up new leadership techniques.

This unfavourable tendency frequently results from an adult being trapped in a childhood conflict over not receiving enough attention from caretakers in the early years of life. The end result is a person who has an excessive need for attention and a drive to stand out or be innovative.

These people experience shame because they believe they are worthless or attention-deprived, which traps them in feelings of loneliness or despair over not being "special" enough to those who matter. As a result, they frequently revolt against those in positions of power whom they perceive to be unreliable. Instead of acting in a proper manner, they start acting rebelliously and provocatively, tricking people into supporting their brilliant schemes. Exaggeration of the truth to the point of fantasy; blatant self-promotion and self-aggrandizement; excessive talking to dominate others; pontificating and inventing elaborate stories; disrespect for authority figures; disregard for laws that run counter to their goals; an automatic rejection of other people's ideas; an insatiable need to be the centre of attention; and a terminal individualism, uniqueness, or novelty.

In some respects, the external appearance is exceptionally severe. Results in a volatile environment working with these disruptive leaders is difficult because they seek attention but don't want the limitations that come with being in the spotlight. It may be quite unpleasant for them when they are in the spotlight since they often implicitly doubt their own ability to impress. They therefore lure attention, start engaging in excessive behaviour, and then deflect the attention that follows. They are unpredictable due to this pattern, which causes chaos and confusion for others around them.

Acting or speaking in a way that suggests, "None of this is my responsibility!" Excessive personal responsibility-based conflict avoidance. This damaging behaviour is a result of a childhood issue with not receiving enough acceptance and approval. As a result, there is an obsessive need to win everyone's favour, including that of total strangers. The inside dread is that one would be shunned or mocked as unlovable by important people.

They feel helpless and undeserving of attention because they believe that others find them undesirable. This may be a traumatic experience, and since they don't think they deserve it, they can't express their needs or ask others for what they want. They submit to people in positions of power and suffer covertly from dependency, pessimism, and the stigma of being "needy" for even the smallest amount of acceptance.

Would you like to have a look for these signs of this poisonous leadership style?

Toxic leadership is a style of management that is harmful to team members and the workplace as a whole. The leader selfishly abuses his or her position of authority. It's tough for you and your peers to flourish when the leadership is poisonous. Usually, a toxic leader has their own self-interest at heart. This has varying degrees of impact on a team's productivity, morale, and performance.

Complaining, blaming, and slandering others; dissatisfied resentment of those in authority; ceding control and becoming dependent on others; coming across as "needy" and draining; asking others to make decisions and then resenting it; avoiding leadership to avoid responsibility later; unintentionally inviting others to dominate them; blaming others for being the "bully"; unwillingness to accept responsibility; desire to be "nice" or "good" in an atmosphere where conflict is avoided; Working with these destructive leaders can be difficult since they expend a lot of energy caring for or assisting people with an unspoken expectation that they will receive something in return. For instance, they may provide care with the understanding that the individual will be in charge of making decisions.

However, they might not express this expectation to the other party. Because they don't want to take responsibility for any negative effects, there is an unintentional redirection of blame. In doing so, they may continue to defend their acts and maintain their "good" or "innocent" persona. In order for them to escape responsibility, this behaviour fosters a culture of resentful finger-pointing and undermines their purpose, their leaders, and others.

Expressions or actions that suggest, "Just do what I say!" Excessive power over others that ignores their humanity. This harmful behaviour is the result of a childhood conflict about having insufficient autonomy and control over one's environment due to oppressive authority figures. This conundrum leads to an obsession with power and an obsessive desire to rule over or even objectify people.

They treat other people like manipulable objects rather than as valuable humans who can further their goals. They frequently don't make the effort to cultivate deep connections. They don't want to be viewed as weak or defenseless. They want to be the great hero who saves others because they need to feel powerful, but their true motivation is to defend themselves from a deep-seated fear of vulnerability. They eventually become enraged at anyone who exhibits any evidence of frailty or being human in any manner, preferring to exhibit unstoppable vitality that is unstoppable.

Dismissing others as unimportant to their goals; frequently getting frustrated with others' slowness; disregarding others' values or needs; appearing cold to others' concerns; appearing unable to sit still long enough for a two-way conversation; appearing unable to be quiet long enough to hear others; and believing that they are better than others. Have faith in themselves as courageous warriors who will protect the helpless.

Demands for devotion at any cost in exchange for protection. Working with these damaging leaders is difficult because they require unwavering commitment. They will use their might to keep people safe, but in exchange, they want complete submission. They neglect moral principles that could stand in their way, and they anticipate that people around them will do the same. They are hostile to anyone who exhibits any sort of lack of allegiance. Disloyal people are swiftly rejected and ignored. Disloyal people are swiftly rejected and ignored. There is no "in-between," you are either "in" or "out."

"Believe me; I'm always right." Excessively dismissing others and mocking their ignorance. This harmful leadership style is influenced by a childhood conflict over not being intelligent enough to make reasonable decisions because authoritative people continually undervalue them. This leads to excessive status-seeking and a drive to be respected by other people. Being viewed as unimportant, which hurts because it indicates that you are inferior to others or insufficient, is the source of inner anxiety. One has strong sentiments of inadequacy when one is "less than." This is unbearable to them, so they exert every effort to get credentials that will serve as evidence of their success on the outside. They never forgets mistakes; interrupts others to point out errors before they have finished speaking; is unable to rely on people who cannot meet their standards; comes across as distant and unapproachable; exhibits excessive and obsessive perfectionism.

You might want to exercise caution if you see these tendencies in your present leadership team. Always keep in mind that toxic leaders are not only disagreeable. They deliberately put their own interests ahead of those of others. This self-focus may be a sign that they don't want to change, but it does not imply that they are incapable of changing because everyone has the capacity to change if they so desire.

You may tell when someone is using you to allay their irrational worries by understanding their intentions. With this understanding, you may design a plan for dealing with them that limits harm to you. If that isn't possible, you can start planning your leave or, if necessary, move to a different boss or business. You are not alone if you have already considered leaving your company due to one of these bosses.

There is yet hope if you recognise any of these indicators in yourself. The majority of people can relate to one or both of these tendencies. But if they go out of control, you and everyone else will suffer. Even if destructive practises are not sustainable over the long term, they may result in quick victories.

Quick gains come at a significant cost and are likely to backfire later, despite the fact that they may seem "correct" today. With conscious growth, you may overcome these fear-based habits if you are aware of your inclinations. If you want to improve as a leader, you may decide to stop letting fear dictate your course of action and choices.

Criticism of authority and whistleblowing from a moralistic perspective. Viewing people as ignorant fools. Being too critical of anything that is not ideal. Establishing unattainable standards that no one can meet These damaging leaders are difficult to work with because they set standards so high that the environment becomes stagnant. Working with these damaging leaders is difficult because they have impossible expectations that no one can ever meet. An unsteady, withheld atmosphere results from people's unquenchable drive to outsmart and disprove their opponents. Everything is seen from a pessimistic angle.

Throwing aside objections right away becomes the norm, which has the unintended effect of making people avoid doing the labour necessary to accomplish everything correctly.

The destructive qualities of a leader (and how to spot them) Working under dysfunctional leadership is challenging on more than just a morale level. An entire team's performance may also be impacted. Because toxic leaders frequently prioritise their personal needs, their actions put the wellbeing of their team at risk. Even if it may seem clear in hindsight, toxic or destructive leaders are not always easy to identify. Let's examine what toxic leadership could include and how to cope with a toxic leader and their poisonous behaviours so that you can succeed at work.

What consequences can toxic leadership have?

Everyone who works with a leader who has toxic leadership or poor leadership abilities is affected. In an investigation by the University of Manchester, 1,200 people were asked about the consequences of toxic leadership, which included: Bullying at work; ineffective conduct at work; job unhappiness; psychological suffering; depression and burnout When toxic leaders are present, workplace bullying frequently develops as a resolving mechanism. Employees are more prone to take revenge and target their resentment at others around them. In general, a toxic boss is a barrier to a positive workplace environment. Of course, not every toxic leader will have the same impact on the workplace culture since not every toxic leader will exhibit the same poisonous attributes.

How can you recognise a toxic leader?

To be able to adapt and succeed in spite of their influence, it's critical to be aware of any potentially toxic leaders in your immediate environment. Here are eight poisonous characteristics that make for poor leadership.

They frequently set contradictory goals. Because it's challenging to comprehend your job when you don't have access to the facts, dishonesty in the workplace is corrosive. Inconsistency and frequently retracting their statements are some traits of toxic leaders. Gaslighting may result from this as well. Let's look at an illustration. Consider the scenario when your manager informs you on Thursday that a task is due on Friday and then chastises you when it isn't finished by the end of the day. They now claim that they had earlier stated that it was due today. This is an instance of professional gaslighting. In a form of psychological manipulation known as gaslighting, one person causes the other to doubt their own judgement or memory.

Everyone has room for improvement, but toxic leaders aren't open to hearing helpful criticism. Their failure to listen to team members' concerns stops the group from developing. Additionally, it implies that a toxic boss persists in their old habits. Here is one instance. You believe that eliminating the daily afternoon meeting for the entire team would be more beneficial. You believe that the majority of conversations could be conducted by email. Your management, nevertheless, won't budge on the matter. They were the ones who suggested this meeting, so they're taking it personally.

Toxic leaders struggle to listen to criticism because they think they are always right, which is one of their many flaws. They don't want to be corrected, and they assume that everyone on their team will take what they say at face value. Consider the following scenario: You are in a meeting when your manager says that the customer requested a certain change. Due to the client's warning, you are aware that this is incorrect. They will either ignore you or scold you for trying to correct them if you try to do so. Hierarchy, or people's positions and responsibilities inside a company, is what gives toxic bosses authority over their workforce. They appreciate this hierarchy because they want to retain this authority. They'll make sure it remains there. For instance, they'll block a plan that would give their team members more freedom to act and decide independently.

Whether these biases are good or bad, toxic leaders frequently have them. They frequently do not engage in inclusive leadership. This might manifest as favouritism toward their friends or as sexism, ageism, racism, homophobia, and other forms of prejudice. Such prejudice may lead to an extremely poisonous work environment. Here's an illustration: The management compliments their friend even though they did a terrible job. On the other side, despite exceeding expectations, the same management is never pleased with your job.

Leaders that are toxic frequently lack confidence. Toxic conduct frequently results from an attempt to overcompensate in this way. They could find it challenging to trust their subordinates if they lack confidence. A boss who lacks confidence could micromanage because they don't trust you to complete a task, as one illustration shows.

This is scarcely true, even if toxic leaders think they are always correct. They frequently make poor choices and find it difficult to carry out their duties successfully. To make up for this conduct and elevate themselves, they will likewise degrade and condemn others. Let's imagine, for illustration's sake, that your manager has trouble managing his time. They wind up pressing your team into making decisions that cause projects to be delayed. In the end, this will have an effect on the team's performance.

Managers that are toxic frequently prioritise their own progress over that of others.But because you want to maintain your work and develop in your career, there is pressure to put up with this conduct. Being the first to challenge a toxic boss is not simple. Because of this, toxic leaders are frequently tolerated for extended periods of time.

A poisonous individual might nevertheless possess charm, which allows them to mask their toxicity. They are hence not always simple to identify. Although they will display some of the aforementioned characteristics, they won't necessarily do it openly or clearly. More subtly than others, certain hazardous actions might be observed.It could be challenging to recognise a toxic leader's masquerade for someone who doesn't interact with them on a daily basis.

An individual cannot defeat a poisonous boss by themselves. That isn't always the case. No one will ever speak up, and the issue won't be handled, if everyone feels they cannot deal with a poisonous boss. Because they are afraid of being alone, many team members accept toxic conduct. But frequently, it just takes one individual who is ready to stand up. When that occurs, other people will have the confidence to speak up as well, and you may begin resolving the problem as a group.

In order to promote their careers, leaders must be poisonous.Since corporate roles are very competitive, many people think they must develop poisonous tendencies in order to "make it." However, toxic leaders exhibit negative traits that are bad for the organisation over the long term. It is possible to advance in your job and be a fantastic leader without becoming toxic.

Leaders that are poisonous occasionally have no idea what they are doing. Their actions may be a coping strategy for their own self-doubts. It follows that some toxic leaders are capable of evolving over time.

Let's examine falsehoods regarding poisonous leaders.

- Your team won't put up with toxic conduct. It's simple to believe that if a leader is toxic, the situation won't last for very long since you and your team won't tolerate it. The best way to handle a toxic leader.
- Try to be helpful rather than critical. Aid others around you in achieving more and generating results. Instead of wasting time on drama, you might concentrate on succeeding as a team. At least you don't have to concentrate on and give the harmful conduct all of your attention if you can't stop it.
- Maintain composure in your replies. Although you have no influence over your manager's actions, you do have power over how you respond to them. Keep in mind that this behaviour isn't directed at you. Keep your emotions under control and refuse to give them the attention they need. Consider approaching your HR department for assistance if you're having trouble handling this on your own.
- Keep track of the requests that your toxic leader makes that you disagree with. In the event of a fallout, you will then be able to demonstrate that you were ordered

to do particular actions that caused the fallout. Prior to carrying out an activity that you disagree with, always request an email confirmation.

- Define limits in the workplace. Maintain a professional connection with your leader. You are not required to get along with your leader or provide personal information. You will shield your personal life from poisonous conduct by doing this. In some circumstances, you can try to control the behaviour by "grey rocking," although this is not advised over the long run.

- Approach your management and have an open dialogue. You can try to have this dialogue, even though toxic leaders won't always be amenable to it. The purpose of an open discussion is not to level accusations but rather to express how you feel and how it is affecting your performance. Use "I" sentences to speak about yourself and the organisation as a whole rather than just yourself. Keep in mind that your performance and happiness have an impact on the business as a whole.

- Make directions clear. Don't assume your toxic leader wants what you think they do. This could cause miscommunications. You should always request clarification (in writing) if there is even the slightest ambiguity.

- Put your work first and put your ego aside. Keep in mind not to personalise things. The actions of a toxic leader do not speak to you or your abilities. Don't attempt to show that you're right and your toxic leader is wrong because you can't.

A leader can be detoxified, but how?

A toxic leader can be made less toxic with your assistance, but it's not always possible. Your manager should be at least receptive to hearing your ideas and accepting helpful feedback. No matter what you do, if your leader is not receptive to this, they won't change. Keep in mind that you don't have to assist someone in changing. Dispelling rumours about harmful leaders Let's examine four falsehoods regarding poisonous leaders.

Your team won't put up with toxic conduct. It's simple to believe that if a leader is toxic, the situation won't last for very long since you and your team won't tolerate it. But because you want to maintain your work and develop in your career, there is pressure to put up with this conduct. Being the first to challenge a toxic boss is not simple. Because of this, toxic leaders are frequently tolerated for extended periods of time.

It's simple to identify toxic leaders. A poisonous individual might nevertheless possess charm, which allows them to mask their toxicity. As a result, they are not always easy to spot. Although they will display some of the aforementioned characteristics, they won't necessarily do so openly or clearly. More subtly than others, certain hazardous actions might be observed. It could be challenging to recognise a toxic leader's mask for someone who doesn't interact with them on a daily basis.

A single person cannot defeat a poison boss on their own. That isn't always the case. No one will ever speak up, and the issue won't be handled, if everyone feels they cannot deal with a poisonous boss. Because they are afraid of being alone, many team members accept toxic behaviour. But frequently, it just takes one individual who is ready to stand up. When that occurs, other people will have the confidence to speak up as well, and you may begin resolving the problem as a group.

In order to promote their careers, leaders must be poisonous. Since corporate roles are very competitive, many people think they must develop poisonous tendencies in order to "make it." However, toxic leaders exhibit negative traits that are bad for the organisation over the long term. It is possible to advance in your job and be a fantastic leader without becoming toxic.

Negative individuals are necessarily toxic leaders. Leaders that are poisonous occasionally have no idea what they are doing. Their actions may be a coping strategy for their own self-doubts. It follows that some toxic leaders are capable of evolving over time.

Lead the way

Sticks everywhere; no carrots management seldom provides positive feedback for what is going well, instead concentrating only on what staff are doing incorrectly or fixing issues. or largely rewards top performance and punishes everyone else; the encroaching red tape With a concentrated concentration on micromanaging personnel, there are too many levels of permission and supervision to get things done. Bullies rule the roost: a concentrated concentration on profits, outperforming the competition, and expense reduction without regard for other bottom lines. Losing the human touch; bullying of employees by management; or the tolerance of management when bullying happens among employees.

High levels of stress, turnover, absenteeism, and burnout; the establishment of internal competition among employees enforced by a performance assessment system that places an emphasis on individual performance rather than team performance; little to no consideration for work-life balance, where a personal life takes precedence over a professional life; overwork or workaholism, which is frequently demonstrated by 50-hour workweeks or longer, little to no vacation time, and availability for work communications around the clock; little evidence of leaders' compassion and empathy for employees; little or no commitment to making contributions to the community, deserving causes, or improving the world. Workplace decorum has declined, and bullying has become more prevalent. The toxic leaders that occupy these environments have an obvious symbiotic relationship with them.

Organisational implications

In the near term, toxic leaders may be successful and advantageous to the company. Their success is typically fleeting before they are compelled to transfer to another school since they are unable to produce effective leaders or cohesive teams. Therefore, businesses need a system in place for detecting toxic leaders and either monitoring them or getting rid of them.

The majority of healthcare organisations use a top-down performance review system, which enables such a leader to not only quash any criticism but also advance up the leadership ladder. Their actions have a variety of effects on the organisation. Toxic leaders undermine the self-worth, dignity, and "psychosocial well-being" of employees in place of honest and supportive leadership. Employee disengagement or active disengagement lowers morale and negatively affects production and efficiency. Employees who work for this boss may be too shy or afraid to express their opinions. The stress of scrutinising every word while attempting to survive in a toxic society on a daily basis leads to a loss of creativity.

The connections among academics or peers degrade as they become more isolated, with the exception of those who are favoured by the leader. Unproductive teams struggle to effectively handle the typical daily conflict, which leads to lower resilience, accelerated burnout, and high turnover.

Although this conduct destroys the workplace culture, it can be hard for the leader's supervisor to see it since these leaders typically present as strong and authoritative, yet they frequently engage in what is known as the "dark triad."

Both behavioural issues and deeper psychological issues can contribute to toxic leadership. There are various phases involved in toxic leader management strategies. The following supervisory and managerial behaviours are appropriate for toxic leaders' peers and subordinates: Pay attention. Demonstrate empathy.

• Provide victims with therapy.

• Keep repeating your key principles.

• Create a hotline so that terrified workers may report abusive conduct.

• Create a hotline so that terrified workers may report abusive conduct.

• Demand that actions and fabrications be documented.

• Inform employees that they should not have alone conversations.

• Offer peer recognition and incentive schemes.

• Promote alliances.

• Lead team-building activities.

• Involve human resources and, if required, the legal division.

• Deal with behavior's changeable causes, such as substance abuse, problems in personal relationships, or physical or mental illness.

• Clearly state the impact of the conduct on others, promote change, and keep an eye on the results.

• Invite an unbiased outsider to assess the workplace.

• Assist with 360-degree behaviour assessments.

• They require coaching.

• Request that the leader take accountability.

Involving HR staff in the process is the first step since they may be able to collect the essential data from all sources. Other transient circumstances or stressful ones not related to work might also be the cause of the behaviour. The troubled leader will probably want concrete instances of the problematic actions. It's possible for leaders to lack self-awareness and be shocked to see how toxic the culture has become as a result of their actions. When senior management shows a commitment to tackling it rather than turning a blind eye, certain leaders may see the issue or reap the benefits. The CEO, physician supervisor, or administrator should not pass judgement on the leader and should instead provide HR support and guidance. The manager can tell whether a leader is denying responsibility or accepting it. The leader must next consider potential repercussions, get a deadline, and get instructions on particular actions to take that will be observed.

HR should maintain the intervention and track its success until certain benchmarks are reached. Additionally, the leader should be urged to maintain relationships within standard professional norms. When supervisors become aware of the conduct, they have an obligation to provide supervised peers, trainees, and workers with a non-threatening setting where they may voice their concerns. It bears emphasising that HR should be included in all phases of any recommendations or actions. If required, the intervention escalates from a casual awareness meeting through disciplinary action. The supervisor may suggest therapy and a 360-degree feedback survey if the leader does not alter his or her behaviour after receiving many warnings. A 360-degree feedback survey asks for input on the employee from a variety of sources, including supervisors, peers, direct reports, and self-evaluations. The DISC-Behavior Styles Purpose is a frequently employed tool in this area (drive, influence, steadiness, and compliance). This gives feedback on behaviour and emotions but does not assess IQ or abilities.

A huge private health system's specialist section flourished because of the positive interactions between the hired physicians and personnel but was constrained by subpar financial results. Thereafter, a new division leader was sought for a year. Despite the formation of a search committee made up of doctors, nurses, and office workers, earlier hires in this and other disciplines sometimes depended on the whim of the department head. The chosen applicant had impeccable manners and charisma during the interview. Despite several medical interviewers' reservations about the candidate's brief employment at his two past companies and the scant information supplied by those employers, the physician was hired for the position.

The division's culture quickly degraded within six months. Initial unhappiness among the instructors, trainees, and staff was seen and was based on intimidation, deceitful conduct, a lack of compassion for the workers, and a lack of accountability for bad choices. Over the course of three years, the division boss was the target of several complaints made to human resources. These were fired by the department head, perhaps in large part due to the division's better financial situation over the previous 36 months.

The department chair requested the division chief's resignation after four years and a sizable number of official complaints to human resources. Task-focused executives, particularly those starting new positions, may be given specific assignments with deadlines to address issues like financial shortages, like in this instance. Almost to the exclusion of other factors, including the relationship component, the new leader could be single-minded in his or her pursuit of the department head's directives.

It is just as important to know how goals are met as what is accomplished. Although there were financial benefits in this case, they came at a great cost to the team's supportive culture and psychological safety. Additionally, for almost four years, the built-in safeguards—HR and the director's supervisor—failed in this case. Because of the director's authoritarian behaviour, which included bullying, aggressiveness, intimidation, and manipulation, the workplace became poisonous.

Confronting false allegations and taking credit for the team's accomplishments are two more behaviours that may be present. These leaders have a "kiss up and kick down proclivity" as well. Why are people who foster such poisonous environments permitted, given the harm they cause to organisations? Most of the time, bosses are concerned with achieving predetermined metrics, while subordinates fear reprisal if they raise issues (e.g., research dollars, clinical revenue). In this instance, the person improved the organisation's financial situation, albeit at a hefty expense.

Supervisors allow bad conduct to continue while passively monitoring it without calling for change. The regulations that the HR department must follow may entail the verification of complaints, internal investigations, placing the person on a performance plan, or involving a coach over a period of months prior to the recommendation to terminate employment. Moreover, top leadership and HR may want to prevent the possibility of legal action, including dismissal, without a solid track record of verified complaints and evaluations. Due to the division's current profitability, there may potentially be conflicts between the department and the health system.

How can a micromanager be identified?

Burnout and despair are prevalent among their employees. Micromanagers are managers who strive to control every detail of the business, project, activity, or anything else it may be, no matter how minor. Bullying, micromanagement, and exclusivity are likely to lead to more worker burnout and high-strung emotions. They could unintentionally give their staff an impossible-to-manage and unsupportable task if their bosses are toxic. Disengagement and burnout can also be caused by these excessive workloads.

If a leader appears to be micromanaging, there may be a problem with control or trust. Start by addressing the source of their lack of trust in their staff by asking them why.

It's nearly a guarantee that every business will at some point come across executives who behave in a poisonous way. Establishing accountability today will be crucial for assisting those leaders in evolving, improving, and changing for the better in the future. All humans go through a process known as personality development, which includes a person's modes of thinking, feeling, and acting. It is impacted by the interaction of genetics and life experience. As a result, there is a lot of variation in personality, emotional intelligence, the use of adult and immature protection mechanisms, and interpersonal styles from person to person. No one is exempt from acquiring characteristics that would be considered maladaptive, not even someone aspiring to a leadership position.

Leaders that prioritise hierarchy and elevate their friends or former coworkers above those with comparable qualifications foster exclusivity and an "in group/out group" mentality. The "in group" is hence frequently given preferential treatment and held to various standards. Even for members of the "in group," this is never a good idea. An open and equitable workplace culture actively seeks out different viewpoints and opinions. If you observe the contrary occurring in your workplace, call attention to it and remind your boss of the value of inclusion for everyone and the general wellbeing of the organisation. Give them concrete next steps to take, including promoting one-on-one meetings with less chatty staff members or provoking dialogue with more talkative staff members during company events.

They are developing a cronyism culture. If there is a feeling of exclusivity, your leader can be toxic. Sometimes managers who favour some staff members over others might unintentionally or intentionally foster exclusivity and cliques. Even worse, some bosses construct "in groups" and "out groups" using the company's ideals, which is never acceptable.

Even with explicitly defined principles, beliefs, and practises, Evans contends that there should be room for people with various life experiences, perspectives, and backgrounds.

Here are some examples of how managers may be unknowingly contributing to a toxic workplace. The values, behaviours, and beliefs that will support the business cultures that leaders hope to develop must be defined and articulated. And for a variety of reasons, leaders might fail to keep these cultures alive. They may be suffering from unrestrained narcissism if they prioritise their own demands for respect, admiration, and approval over those of their employees and the goals of the business. Or perhaps they lead in a way that instils fear; they engage in behaviours that make others feel unsafe and afraid at work. These leaders often make others feel inferior in order to feel powerful. Chris Evans, CEO of Barefoot, a brand experience agency on a mission to end meaningless moments between consumers and brands, says that fear of competitors, market changes, and obsolescence can be motivating. If a common enemy is to be profiled, it should be something external to the organisation that ultimately motivates the mission's completion.

Other characteristics of a toxic leader might be hubris, a reluctance to listen and accept criticism, or self-interested decision-making.

The fact of the issue is that we are hypocrites and that toxic leaders and work environments are on the rise. We frequently opt for or adhere to a totally different sort of leader. We employ and promote self-centered autocrats, bullies, psychopaths, and narcissists, whose long-term effects may harm, if not completely destroy, companies (and even countries). In my two decades as an executive coach, I have encountered more of the leaders described in this paragraph than those described in the first paragraph. Because they only consider their success in financial terms or because they add charismatic entertainment value to the business, many people are quick to overlook these toxic leaders and the harm they inflict. In 2010, the Workplace Bullying Institute conducted a survey that found that 35% of American workers, or 53.5 million people, had personally experienced bullying, which is defined as "repeated mistreatment by one or more employees that takes the form of verbal abuse, threats, intimidation, humiliation, or sabotage of work performance." Another 15% of workers reported having witnessed bullying at work. Bosses make up around 72% of those bullies.

Playing on the followers' most basic desires and anxieties; threatening or punishing those who disobey the leader or voice dissent; intentionally misleading the followers; and placing the blame for mistakes or failures on others.

Perhaps no one understands the ageing workforce better than HR professionals, and training younger managers on how to properly manage older employees who report to them is fast becoming a crucial workplace activity. The causes of this occurrence are many. Older people are beginning to return to the workforce as the epidemic that forced many of them out eases. Meanwhile, rising prices and the prospect of a recession have forced many retirees in need of additional money back into the workforce. Many times, their bosses are a decade younger or more than they are. Here are pointers for younger managers who supervise older employees to aid in that effort:

- HR must educate managers on the significance of preventing age discrimination. Over one-third of the workforce is made up of people 50 and older, and 78% of them claim to have experienced age discrimination in some way. Most supervisors are unaware that asking an older worker's age is improper and, in some situations, unlawful. It could be a good idea to remind managers not to ask it.
- Discover the preferred communication method. To interact with employees, several organisations use online platforms like Slack or Flock. But demanding the use of those gadgets might result in misunderstandings for certain elderly workers who might not be adept with cellphones. I would advise asking about the preferences of elderly employees. Or, if the business makes extensive use of such channels for communication, offer assistance and training.
- Younger managers can use LinkedIn or other social networking sites to conduct online research on the older

employees who report to them to find out what they may have in common. However, they should treat such material with care and confirm that workers are okay with having their prior successes examined on social media.

- Respect is especially important for older workers, who deserve it. Jones claims that many of them have been with the company for many years and are a wealth of information. What is the company's greatest chance for development, according to the best questions to ask? and "What is the biggest vulnerability of the company?"

- According to a recent AARP poll, around 3 out of 5 baby boomers indicate they wish to acquire new skill sets. According to me, these Boomers often rate among the most engaged workers, so investing time and money to teach them is well worth it. I also advise younger managers to "explicitly ask them what skill set they want to be leading with."

- Younger managers can greatly benefit from the insider information that many older employees have to provide. Use the corporate wisdom of more experienced employees before speaking up in any meetings, I urgednew managers, and you won't be sorry.

- Asking senior employees about their own objectives and aspirations is very beneficial for younger supervisors. According to me, some people will be more task-oriented, while others will be more relationship-focused. However, it's crucial to determine who wants what. Who is the finest leader you have ever worked with, and why? is a great question to ask when you meet with them.

- Some older workers, like any other worker, may approach their findings differently. Let them know that they have the space to choose the strategy they like. However, an older employee posted sticky notes on a wall asking for contributions. The secret to success when dealing with an older employee and a younger boss is to act like a manager rather than always like a good friend.

- Both younger managers and older staff will make mistakes when working together. Perhaps someone old enough to be your grandma will perceive the world a little bit differently from you. However, she said, finding an excellent mentor among the more experienced employees and allowing those individuals to advise the younger manager may be quite valuable.

- If an employee quits soon after attending training sessions that cost a lot of money, employers could believe their investment was a waste. However, there are several legal dangers to consider before implementing that sort of policy. Some companies demand that employees reimburse them for the expense of training in that circumstance.

Recovering training expenses is acceptable if the training is voluntary, relates to work skills, and the employment contract calls for reimbursement of training expenses in the event that an employee quits their position within a specific time frame. When an employee is hired or just before the training begins, employers can get written permission from them to recover the expenses of voluntary training. Making the wrong choice about training expenses may result in troublesome lawsuits for businesses. They could get into a wage and hour dispute with that worker. It could make more of a mess than it would cost to pay for that training.

In addition to the legal implications, attempting to extort money from someone who may not have any is a waste of time. The same difficulties confronted by any creditor trying to collect on a debt exist for employers even though they may be legally allowed to pursue recovery of the training expenditures. The employee might not have the funds to pay, and sometimes the expense of trying to collect makes the procedure impossible. The employer must determine whether it makes sense to seek collection through lawsuit if the employee lacks the funds to pay. Litigation is frequently not necessary. Employers can get around this issue by deferring paying employees' training expenses up front and only paying them back after the individual has been working at the position for a specific period of time. Occasionally, companies deduct the entire training cost from the employee's final paycheck.

Performance evaluations might not be the most enjoyable aspect of the work, but when the year comes to a conclusion, they are unavoidable. Experts offered guidance for managers who would be conducting the reviews as well as ideas for improving firms' manager training programmes. More than 4 in 10 CEOs identified the potential disparities between remote and in-office employees as their top worry in a study of 10,000 white-collar workers done by Future Forum, a research consortium founded by Slack, according to a March article on SHRM Online. Additionally, Chamberlin said that 2021 research conducted in the United Kingdom "found remote workers felt more pressure, worked longer hours, yet were less than half as likely to get promoted, and just 38% earned a bonus." Nonetheless, strengthening relationships between staff members and supervisors is critical to eliminating proximity bias and ensuring that work is judged consistently regardless of location.

The most important piece of advice for keeping impartial and avoiding proximity bias during performance evaluations is to implement manager training, define objective performance measures, and use performance management software. Proximity bias arises because managers need to make it a regular practise to check in with all employees, not just the ones they meet in person, and they might not be basing their performance evaluations on objective measuring techniques. It's reasonable for individuals to acquire biases in favour of the people they make connections with, but it shouldn't lead to biassed reviews.

Being vague is one of the most pointless things a manager can do, according to her. They shouldn't offer general comments like "You could do better" or "Good work." Without direction, the employee will be unsure of how to advance.

Training for managers is essential. This is particularly important for new managers "so that they learn to communicate more effectively, increase employee performance in real time, coach staff to accomplish their objectives and key achievements, and conduct fair reviews based on actual objective performance data." HR should provide managers with technologies that enable weekly one-on-one digital check-ins for remote workers as well as define and monitor objective performance criteria, such as objectives and important results, that they can use as a guide when composing reports. According to Chamberlin, " a lot of leaders use data and staff output in addition to their personal presence to assess work and areas for improvement." If a manager hasn't completed rigorous leadership training that shows the possibility of proximity bias and how to prevent it, leading and assessing in this new style may be neglected.

Don't just assume that your staff members will appreciate the training and professional development opportunities you provide for them. Share with them the benefits of training, both now and in the future.

As a leader, you must prioritise the creation of a positive workplace culture. Culture will alter and evolve; therefore, it's important to monitor it and make adjustments as needed. The components of a toxic work environment may occasionally be obvious and simple to change, but they may also be concealed, in which case leaders must consistently endeavour to find them.

About The Author

Dr. Amit Das, is a renowned executive advisor, consultant, educationist, author, speaker, counsellor, and coach whose 25+ years of business experience provides high-impact, practical solutions that support his clients' leadership development and organisational transformations. He worked for fortune 500 companies and left rich leagacy of organising transformational learning workshops. He has transformed more than 5000+ working executives through his path breaking capability building learning workshops. Dr. Amit Das is recognised as an innovative, principled thought leader who combines intellectual rigor and discipline with an ability to translate theory into practice. His operational skills are coupled with a strategic ability to analyse, develop, and implement successful strategies for profitability, growth, and sustainability.

Dr. Amit Das has a successful track record in aligning learning and training solutions to key business strategy with a strong focus on flawless execution excellence to facilitate individual, business divisional, and organisational performance. He keeps relentless focus on measuring training impact and ROI, people capability building graphs, training process governance, performance coaching, and strategic thinking. These have been some of his key individual success traits. His core capabilities include performance coaching, designing training and development frameworks, psychometric assessment and analysis, competency framework development and assessments, content design and facilitation of soft skills and leadership programmes, Learning Management Systems, Learning Impact Measurement, Talent Analysis, and Performance Coaching and Counselling.

Dr. Amit Das has authored multiple management and self-development books, like Akrasia to Enkrateia, You Are Born To Succeed, Reinventing and Redefining You, Change Your Perspective Change Your Life, 90 Minutes Mindfulness, The Alchemy Of Resilient Leadership, Redefining Organisational Excellence, High Impact Leadership, A Divorce-Free Married Life, Redefining Corporate Spectrum, Create Your Leadership Edge, Love-Laugh- Live With Happiness, SMART Parenting @ Zero Cost, Redefining HRM, Building Organisational Capability, Ethical Road Map, Attomic Attention, BYPB, Redefining The Power Of Mentoring, Making The Most Future Fit Organisation, Redefining Talent Management, Defining Your Success Factors, Lead or Plead, Make The Most Of Your Life, Better Half or Bitter Half, Psychology Of Learning And Development, The Transformative Mind & Soul are few of them.

He has a Ph.D. and a Fellowship in strategic learning, along with his first class degrees in Human Resource Management, Marketing Management, International Business, and Corporate Laws from the top business schools in India. He is a certified Psychometric analyst, HR Analyst, OD Interventionist, Human Psychologist, Lifecoach, Leadership Developer, Black Belt (LSS), Strategic Thinker, Talent Analyst, certified professional trainer and certified behavioral coach.

Dr. Amit Das teaches courses related to Organisational Development, Human Resource Management, Self-Management, and Leadership Coaching. He regularly engages in consulting and training work for organisation and leadership development with organisations across industries and with many institutions of higher education. He has published many research articles in the fields of human resource management, business compliance at the workplace, mindfulness, the business-society interface, and the best practises in management in reputed journals.

Dr. Amit Das likes googling, reading books, writing articles & books, cooking, listening to old melodies, and counselling people to unleash their true potential to build a strong nation. He is married and blessed with a son. He would love to hear about your experience after reading his books. You can email him and share your thoughts, or you can use his services for life coaching, positive behavioural counseling, educational support, and mentoring for young, promising students pursuing their B.B.A. and M.B.A. degrees. Dr. Amit Das, a leadership consultant by training and occupation, is passionate about writing. He is a firm believer in giving top attention to resolving covert social and psychological goals at work. He aspires to foster a positive workplace atmosphere and uphold improved mental wellness. In order to raise awareness, he plans to write more about these subjects in his next projects.

He enjoys travelling, watching Bollywood & Hollywood movies, and researching a variety of subjects in addition to writing on the aforementioned themes. His insightful, funny, and brutally honest writings about success and failure, self-awareness, and interpersonal relationships have established him as one of the top personal brands. He is an authorpreneur and content producer. The main concepts that have driven his journey—which started with him wanting to be an IIM professor and concluded with him producing material that has been viewed and read by millions—are collected in his book. His opinions cover a wide range of topics, including the value of forming habits for long-term success, the cornerstones of self-management, embracing and accepting failure, and the unvarnished truth about developing empathy. This is a book that you should read and reread, highlight, and ponder over and over again.

References

- *How To Save Your Soul From The Toxic Workplace Paperback – Import, 28 May 2019 by Sheri Young (Author).*
- *Toxic Emotions And The Bottom Line: Keeping Your Workplace Free Of The Emotional Garbage That Can Kill The Bottom Line Of Any Organization! Kindle Edition by Judith Munson (Author).*
- *The Inclusive Leader's Guide to Healthy Workplace Culture: Prevent Toxic Work Environments, Bullying, Sexual Harassment, and Discrimination Paperback – Import, 23 September 2019 by Meredith Holley (Author).*
- *The Highly Sensitive Person's Guide to Dealing with Toxic People: How to Reclaim Your Power from Narcissists and Other Manipulators Kindle Edition by Shahida Arabi MA (Author), Andrea Schneider (Foreword) Format: Kindle Edition.*
- *Toxic Workplace!: Managing Toxic Personalities and Their Systems of Power Hardcover – Illustrated, 29 April 2009 by Mitchell Kusy (Author), Elizabeth Holloway (Author).*
- *Surviving the Toxic Workplace: Protect Yourself Against Coworkers, Bosses, and Work Environments That Poison Your Day (BUSINESS SKILLS AND DEVELOPMENT) Paperback – Import, 16 March 2010 by Linnda Durre (Author).*
- *Toxic: A Guide to Rebuilding Respect and Tolerance in a Hostile Workplace Hardcover – 20 April 2021 by Clive Lewis (Author).*
- *Future Fit: How to Stay Relevant and Competitive in the Future of Work Paperback – Import, 25 May 2021 by*

Andrea Clarke (Author).

- *Made in Future: A Story of Marketing, Media, and Content for our Times Hardcover – Import, 16 May 2022 by Prashant Kumar (Author).*
- *The Future Is Faster Than You Think Paperback – 17 February 2020 by Peter H. Diamandis and Steven Kotler (Author).*
- *Leadership: Theory and practice. Los Angeles, CA: SAGE Publications, Inc by Northouse, P. published 2019.*
- *The Constructivist Leader (Paperback) by Deborah Walker,published 1995.*
- *Credibility: How Leaders Gain and Lose It, Why People Demand It (Paperback) by James M. Kouzes, published 1993.*
- *Appreciative Leadership: Focus on What Works to Drive Winning Performance and Build a Thriving Organization (Hardcover) by Diana Whitney, published 2010.*
- *Thinking, Fast and Slow (Hardcover) by Daniel Kahneman, published 2011.*
- *The Checklist Manifesto: How to Get Things Right (Hardcover) by Atul Gawande, published 2009.*
- *Toxic Emotions And The Bottom Line: Keeping Your Workplace Free Of The Emotional Garbage That Can Kill The Bottom Line Of Any Organization! Kindle Edition by Judith Munson (Author).*
- *Banx Workplace Culture : Identifying and Eliminating Toxic Workplace Cultures [Print Replica] Kindle Edition by The BANX Group (Author), Allison Brooks (Author), Jason Brooks (Author), Amy Clark (Author), Paul Clark (Author).*
- *Managing Anxiety in Toxic Workplaces: How to Navigate Toxic Workplaces Kindle Edition by Joyce Robert (Author).*
- *Surviving the Toxic Workplace: A Practical Resource for*

New Managers in Any Industry Kindle Edition by Michael Huizinga (Author).

- *Guidelines to thrive in a toxic workplace: PART ONE Kindle Edition by Enna Sur (Author).*
- *A Workforce INSPIRED: Tools to Manage Negativity and Support a Toxic-Free Workplace Kindle Edition by Dolores Neira (Author), Kimberly Nash-Amezcua (Author), Cynthia Klein (Author), Victoria Lemus (Author) Format: Kindle Edition.*
- *The Drama-Free Workplace: How You Can Prevent Unconscious Bias, Sexual Harassment, Ethics Lapses, and Inspire a Healthy Culture Kindle Edition by Patti Perez (Author) Format: Kindle Edition.*
- *Seeking Civility: How Leaders, Managers & HR Can Create a Workplace Free of Bullying Kindle Edition by Catherine Mattice (Author).*
- *The simple strategies of effectively working with others.: Collaborating with colleagues, clientele, supervisors, or employees to establish a stress-free work environment. Kindle Edition by Stephen Rowling (Author).*
- *Toxic Leaders: Are They Poisoning Your Workplace? Paperback – Import, 3 August 2017 by Gianna C Clark (Author).*
- *Leverage Leadership: A Practical Guide to Building Exceptional Schools (Paperback) by Doug Lemov, published 2012.*
- *Rethinking Leadership: A Collection of Articles (Paperback) by Thomas J. Sergiovanni (Editor), published 1999.*
- *Leadership on the Line, With a New Preface: Staying Alive Through the Dangers of Change (Kindle Edition) by Ronald A. Heifetz.*
- *We Want to Do More Than Survive: Abolitionist Teaching*

and the Pursuit of Educational Freedom (Hardcover) by Bettina L. Love, published 2019.

- *Solving Tough Problems: An Open Way of Talking, Listening, and Creating New Realities (Hardcover) by Adam Kahane (Goodreads Author), published 2004.*
- *Change the World: How Ordinary People Can Accomplish Extraordinary Things (Hardcover) by Robert E. Quinn (Goodreads Author), published 2000.*
- *Practical Approaches to Marketing Analytics in the Digital Age (ebook) by Cesar A. Brea, published 2012.*
- *The Innovative University: Changing the DNA of Higher Education from the Inside Out (Hardcover)by Clayton M. Christensen, published 2011.*
- *Reinventing Higher Education: The Promise of Innovation (Hardcover) by Ben Wildavsky (Editor), published 2011.*
- *Bass & Stogdill's Handbook of Leadership: Theory, Research & Managerial Applications (Hardcover) by Bernard M. Bass, published 1990.*
- *The practice of Adaptive Leadership: Tools and Tactics for Changing Your Organization and the world (Hardcover) by Ronald A. Heifetz, published 2009.*
- *The Third Side: Why We Fight and How We Can Stop (Paperback) by William Ury, published 2000.*
- *Accelerate: Building Strategic Agility for a Faster-Moving World (Hardcover) by John P. Kotter (Goodreads Author), published 2012.*
- *How Colleges Change: Understanding, Leading, and Enacting Change (ebook) by Adrianna Kezar, published 2013.*
- *Adaptation Studies and Learning: New Frontiers (Paperback) by Laurence Raw, published 2013*
- *More Than 50 Ways to Build Team Consensus (Paperback) by R. Bruce Williams, published 1993.*

- *Adaptability: Responding Effectively to Change (Paperback) by Allan Calarco, published 2006*
- *Building Resiliency: How to Thrive in Times of Change (Paperback) by Mary Lynn Pulley, published 2001.*
- *Playing to Win: How Strategy Really Works (Hardcover) by A.G. Lafley, published 2013*
- *Leadership Without Easy Answers (Hardcover) by Ronald A. Heifetz, published 1994.*
- *Influencer: The Power to Change Anything (Hardcover) by Kerry Patterson, published 2007*
- *Leadership on the Line: Staying Alive Through the Dangers of Leading (Hardcover)by Ronald A. Heifetz , published 2002.*
- *What To Do When You Are In A Toxic Workplace?: Step-By-Step Guide To Tame A Toxic Workplace: How To Fix A Toxic Workplace Kindle Edition by Antoinette Hasenbeck (Author).*
- *Get Out Of A Toxic Workplace: Strategies For Coping With A Toxic Work Environment: How To Fix Toxic Work Environment Kindle Edition by Jasper Kooker (Author).*
- *Overcome Toxic Workplace: Advice For Assessing The Issues And Dealing With Difficult People: Toxic Co Worker Kindle Edition by Leonore Page (Author).*
- *Toxic Femininity in the Workplace: Office Gender Politics Are a Battlefield Hardcover – Illustrated, 10 September 2019 by Ginny Hogan (Author).*
- *Toxic Workplace: A Guide To Understanding The Working Environment And Overcoming Negative Emotions: Corporate World Kindle Edition by Lurlene Olden (Author).*
- *Surfing on a Toxic Workplace: A Realistic Picture of the World of Work, the Solutions to Survive Bad Leaders and a Strategy for a Future of Well-Being Kindle Edition by*

Matthew K. Atkins (Author).

- *How To Survive In The Toxic Workplace: Taking Care of Yourself in an Unhealthy Environment Kindle Edition by Vishal Mondkar (Author).*
- *The 12 Disorders of The Toxic Workplace: Finding, Facing, and Fixing the Problems That Are Keeping Your Business From Moving Forward Kindle Edition by Carl Prude Jr. (Author).*
- *TOXIC PEOPLE Paperback – 13 May 2021 by Tim Cantopher (Author).*
- *BUDDHA AT WORK Paperback – 19 July 2017 by Geetanjali Pandit (Author).*
- *Breathless: A Survivor's Guide to Thriving in Toxic Workplaces Kindle Edition by Nina Alexander (Author).*
- *Getting Along: How to Work with Anyone (Even Difficult People) Hardcover – Import, 5 December 2022 by Amy Gallo (Author).*
- *Workplace Bullying: How to Navigate a Toxic Workplace Environment Kindle Edition by Barbara F. Boulet (Author).*
- *We've All Done It: Getting Real About the Role We Each Play in a Toxic Workplace Kindle Edition by Kimberly J Benoit (Author).*
- *The Antidote: Building Insanely Profitable, High-Performing Teams Without Creating a Toxic Workplace That Makes People Want to Kill Themselves Kindle Edition by Benjamin Lueck (Author).*
- *From Chaos to Confidence: Your Survival Strategies for the New Workplace Paperback – Import, 5 July 1996 by Susan Campbell (Author).*
- *Toxic Workplaces: From Hurt to Healing Kindle Edition by Anna Remijn Derham (Author).*
- *Overcome Toxic Workplace: Advice For Assessing The*

Issues And Dealing With Difficult People: Signs And Symptoms Of A Toxic Workplace Paperback – Import, 5 August 2021 by Mark Eiken (Author).

- *Workplace Anxiety: How to Deal With Stress, Conflict, Toxic Coworkers and Bosses, and Fear of Losing Your Jo Kindle Edition by David Leads (Author), Relationship Up (Author) Format: Kindle Edition.*
- *Organizational Toxin Handlers: The Critical Role of HR, OD, and Coaching Practitioners in Managing Toxic Workplace Situations Hardcover – Import, 5 September 2020 by Teresa A. Daniel (Author), Lynn Harrison (Foreword).*
- *Toxic Work Environment, Managing Office Politics, Toxic PeToxic Workplace Signs; A Survival Guide How to Survive & Rise Above a Toxic Work Environment, Managing Office Politics, Toxic Personalities, Behaviors, Toxic Coworkers, Bosses, Employees, and Culture by Leon Lyons | 28 September 2022.*
- *Toxic Cultures at Work: The Eight Drivers of a Toxic Culture and a Process for Change by James Cannon | 30 September 2022.*
- *The Inclusive Leader's Guide to Healthy Workplace Culture: Prevent Toxic Work Environments, Bullying, Sexual Harassment, and Discrimination by Meredith Holley | 23 September 2019.*
- *Corporate Toxicity: What's Killing Companies Today? Toxic Polices, Toxic Work Cultures & Toxic Employees! by Anita L Polite-Wilson PH D | 4 July 2020.*
- *Work Well: Transforming Toxic Environments & Creating Healthy Corporate Culture by D.D. Wegman | 21 May 2019.*
- *Creating A Positive Work Culture: Guide To Building The Company Culture Of Your Dreams: Fix Problematic Areas*

Of Toxic Culture by Jerrold Hubiak | 5 August 2021.

- Toxic Work Environment by Nicole L. Turner | 9 October 2016.
- Get Out Of A Toxic Workplace: Strategies For Coping With A Toxic Work Environment: Toxic Behavior In The Workplace by Sydney Deperro | 5 August 2021.
- Your Own Toxic Work Behaviours (Decency Journey Book 4) by Anna Eliatamby | 16 November 2022.
- Cleansing Moments: Developing Leadership Skills For All Times by Dishan Kamdar | 22 November 2022.
- Toxic Work Environment: Bullying, Harassment, Victimisation, False Allegations by Jamar Whelehan | 5 December 2022.
- Jerks at Work: Toxic Coworkers and What to do About Them by Tessa West | 20 January 2022.
- Swimming Upstream: Parenting Girls for Resilience in a Toxic Culture by Laura Choate | 1 October 2015.
- Breakthrough: A Memoir of Toxic Work, Mindfulness, and Inner Peace by Sunita Devi Alves | 26 November 2022.
- Patterns of Work Culture: Cases and Strategies for Culture Building by Jai B.P. Sinha | 6 June 2000.
- Toxic: A Guide to Rebuilding Respect and Tolerance in a Hostile Workplace by Clive Lewis OBE DL | 18 February 2021.
- Principles: How to Create a Principled Business Culture by Sid Mickle | 14 October 2021.
- Rising Above a Toxic Workplace: Taking Care of Yourself in an Unhealthy Environment by Gary Chapman , Paul White , et al. | 1 September 2014.
- Breathless: A Survivor's Guide to Thriving in Toxic Workplaces by Nina Alexander | 3 January 2023.
- The Trouble with Trauma at Work: Tackle Trauma, Foster Psychological Safety and Boost Happiness at Work by K

Howard | 16 February 2023.

- *Create Wealth by Creating High-Performance Teams: 12 Simple Steps To Transform Toxic Teams Into Trusting & Productive Teams by Kamalini Roy | 19 April 2021.*
- *Organizational Development Essentials You Always Wanted To Know by Ankur Mithal and Vibrant Publishers | 17 January 2023.*
- *Technically Wrong – Sexist Apps, Biased Algorithms, and Other Threats of Toxic Tech by Sara Wachter–boettch | 16 October 2018.*
- *The Reset: Ideas to change how we work and live by Elizabeth Uviebinené | 29 April 2021.*
- *Signs of a Toxic Organization - A Brutal Review of Reality by Karan Dhingra | 10 November 2022.*
- *The Culture Code: The Secrets of Highly Successful Groups by Daniel Coyle, Alex McMorran, et al.*
- *Emotionally Toxic Workplaces by Robin Hill and Tam Hill | 10 November 2013.*
- *Toxic Cultures at Work: The Eight Drivers of a Toxic Culture and a Process for Change by James Cannon | 30 September 2022.*
- *Your Own Toxic Work Behaviours: 4 (Decency Journey) by Anna Eliatamby | 16 November 2022.*
- *Coping in a Toxic Environment: 3 (Decency Journey)by Anna Eliatamby | 16 November 2022.*
- *Create Wealth by Creating High-Performance Teams: 12 Simple Steps To Transform Toxic Teams Into Trusting & Productive Teams by Kamalini Roy | 19 April 2021.*
- *The Inclusive Leader's Guide to Healthy Workplace Culture: Prevent Toxic Work Environments, Bullying, Sexual Harassment, and Discrimination by Meredith Holley | 12 March 2019.*